Pathways to Better Quilting

5 shapes for machine quilt patterns

SALLY TERRY

Located in Paducah, Kentucky, the American Quilter's Society (AQS) is dedicated to promoting the accomplishments of today's quilters. Through its publications and events, AQS strives to honor today's quiltmakers and their work and to inspire future creativity and innovation in quiltmaking.

Editor: Helen Squire
Technical Editor: Cheryl Barnes
Graphic Design: Lynda Smith
Cover Design: Michael Buckingham
Photography: Charles R. Lynch

Published by American Quilter's Society
in cooperation with Golden Threads.

Library of Congress Cataloging-in-Publication Data
Terry, Sally.
Pathways to better quilting : 5 shapes for machine quilt patterns / by Sally Terry
p. cm.
ISBN 1-57432-851-4
1. Patchwork. 2. Quilting. I. Title.

TT835.T38 2004
746.46--dc22

2004006160

Additional copies of this book may be ordered from the American Quilter's Society, PO Box 3290, Paducah, KY 42002-3290; Toll Free: 800-626-5420, or online at www.AQSquilt.com.

Dedication

To my daughter, Sarah, to the friends that I can wrap my arms around, and to God for his incredible blessings along the way.

Acknowledgments

To Golden Threads for unbridled encouragement and support.

To Desirée Clausen and Jan Hall, quilting customers and friends, who graciously allowed me artistic freedom on their quilts.

To my wonderful students for asking all the right questions which helped me develop this method of quilting designs and choosing patterns.

To my family, for helping me find my way in the Golden Age of Quilting.

Table of Contents

Introduction

While teaching beginning students, I discovered that we all have the ability to quilt, yet many students do not know where to find that talent within themselves. This book is meant to give you clues and secrets for finding and tapping your creativity, enabling you to join a very special group of quilters. It does not matter if you quilt by hand, or with a traditional machine, shortarm system, midarm or longarm sewing machine. If you are a beginner, professional quilter, or instructor, you will

- Enjoy using fundamental concepts in order to read and execute quilting patterns you once thought were too complicated to attempt, as you discover the true foundation of quilting.

- Accelerate your learning curve with a seemingly effortless transition to freehand quilting. Renew your confidence and enthusiasm with an amazingly simple step-by-step method.

- Experience the satisfaction of interpreting the quilt with quick and easy designs that creatively enhance the quilt top.

These fundamentals will allow you to enroll in fabulous quilting classes with satisfying results. No longer will you feel hampered by your lack of experience and understanding. Now isn't that a refreshing thought – the freedom to grow and create with endless possibilities.

Pathways to Better Quilting is all about you – it focuses on your individual style, skill, and creative ability. This method celebrates your own comfortable way of doing things – like signing your name or drawing your own style of leaf or heart. Your successful execution of this method will be different from that of your other quilting friends. In fact, you are liberated from ever having to imitate me since the results will be unique to you, allowing your sense of creative design to strengthen.

I thank you for purchasing this book and wish you the very best of everything in quilting. I am by nature a giver, so I share with you my quilting method – a technique you may not have looked at before. Take heart and feel the quilting spirit awaken in you.

It all started with my students. I have been quilting on a longarm machine for five years and have quilted hundreds of quilts. When I started teaching, my beginning quilting students lacked the hand-eye coordination to follow the stitch patterns they loved. I felt I had to develop a simple-to-understand system that would help them execute these patterns. I call it *reading the pattern*.

My brain works in funny ways, and after thinking a lot about the designs, I was able to distill the patterns down to five shapes. The *five shapes of quilting* emerged – five easy-to-accomplish shapes and combinations of shapes from which all quilting patterns are made. I call this the *Language of Quilting*. Using the shapes, you can execute any design, from pattern to freehand to pantograph. This guidebook contains clear instructions for recognizing the shapes and learning the correct way to complete the stroke of each shape.

Students always ask how to choose the correct quilting pattern to place on the quilt. I developed a simple step-by-step process to determine what to quilt where. I call it *interpreting the quilt.*

There are no directions here for pinning, basting, or preparing your quilt for quilting. There are many fine books and magazines with that information. In fact, you may already have many of them in your quilting library. The purpose of this book is simply to share in the joyful passion of quilting when using this long-needed technique.

Keep this guidebook next to your machine, whether you quilt on a longarm, midarm, shortarm, or traditional sewing machine. No matter what type of machine and quilting system you are using, the information will work for you. Refer to it often.

Quilts are as passionate for the maker as they are for the recipient.

Design Evolution. Originally, quilting offered warmth and protection. As quilting evolved so did its beauty. As we continue to thread our needles for hand or machine quilting, our creative touch leads to greater emphasis on the stitching design as it relates to the piecing design. The epitome of this creative drive is the rare whole-cloth quilt, prized for its exquisitely executed elaborate quilting designs on plain fabric.

So, how do the thread designs get there? In earlier times, quilts were a sign of status and social standing, and the pieced tops were taken to *pattern markers*. These artisans' sole business was to determine the wishes of the owners and marry them with magnificent patterns that emphasized the piecing.

This business goes on even today; our pattern markers are now stencil designers, quilt pattern designers, and machine quilters. Moreover, we still need to determine the wishes of the owners and match them up with the appropriate patterns – even if we ourselves are the owners.

How I Got Started. I became a professional longarm quilter and educator by accident and divine intervention. I did not piece. My first quilt remained in my garage sales for ten years. Even my relatives did not want to finish the thing, so it finally ended up at the local Salvation Army store. When I give guild talks, guild members still remember that unfinished quilt top pattern.

When I saw my first longarm machine I said, "I can do that." Five days later I bought one and the most joyous part of my life began.

I had always sewn garments and home décor projects, sometimes for eight hours a day. But, I was not originally a piecer of quilts. For that reason I started quilting with a respect for the piecer and a greater appreciation for the creative choices and intricate workings that go into constructing a quilt top.

I have had countless conversations with beginning machine quilters. We agree that our machines should come with instant pattern creating sensors. It would save a lot of headaches and frustration!

If a quilter starts a quilting business, there are many anxious moments spent worrying about making a high quality product for the customer. When you take into account developing hand-eye coordination, making the right quilting pattern choices for the quilt top, and targeting deadlines for completion – things can get very confusing. I had always shared information about this topic in my beginning machine-quilting classes, and this book can help you get started too.

So take heart,
here is your "pathway."

The Pathways of Stitching

There are thousands of wonderful patterns in books, stencils, pantographs, and templates that you can use for marking on your pieced top. If you have always sent your quilts to someone for quilting, I hope this guidebook will give you the inspiration and confidence to begin to quilt your own projects. If you are hesitant, it just may be that you have not practiced with the right pathways.

It is amazing to me that no matter whether you use a longarm, midarm, shortarm, or traditional sewing machine, my stitching concepts apply to all methods of quilting.The following pathways will enable all of you to quickly and easily stitch any design on the quilt sandwich:

Executing any quilting motif

- Read the pattern
- Practice hand-eye coordination
- Train eyes to focus ahead
- Develop smooth strokes
- Count for overall size consistency

Utilizing your creative sense

- Shrink or enlarge patterns
- Transfer patterns
- Develop your own freehand style
- Think with your needle
- Creatively interpret the quilting design

Visualizing the finished quilt

- Gradually audition patterns
- Develop a signature freehand meander
- Incorporate your signature style

The Five Shapes of the Language of Quilting

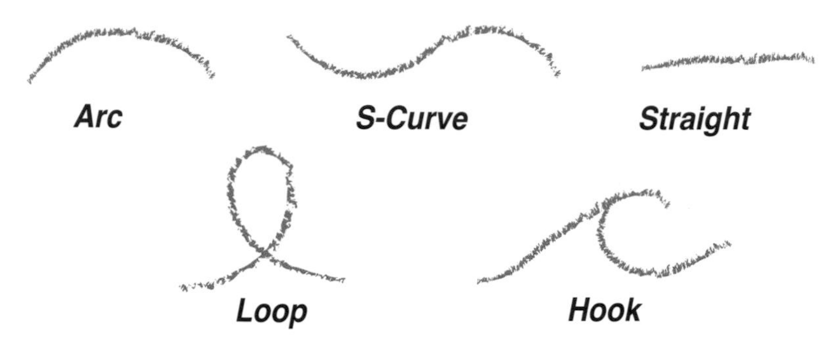

Once you gain mastery of the *Five Shapes of the Language of Quilting,* the possibilities are endless. You are no longer limited to using only stencils or published patterns.

You will begin finding design inspiration from magazine pictures, china patterns, designs on tote bags, lines in the sand, or in graphic designs. Save these inspirations. I have doodles on scrap paper, flimsy napkins from a host of airplane trips, paper cups, and more, all stored in notebooks waiting to be transformed into thread designs.

When looking for a design, we become "super aware" of the idea/pattern we are looking to find. Carry a notebook wherever you go to capture your ideas.

There is no holding back now!

Finding Your Creative Potential

We all have tremendous creative potential within us, so get ready to be encouraged and inspired. It is my job to show you where to find the talent within you!

The best way to start is to warm up. Warm up to the idea you can do it. Warm up to the right side of your brain, which is the creative, thinking side of your brain. Give yourself the opportunity and time for the transition to take place. I light candles and put on music. I love classical music for inspiration and for its mathematically perfect meter. It keeps the left side of your brain quietly busy and relaxed so the right side can create. Then if I really need to get something done, I listen to the Pointer Sisters!

Warming up to the ideas with doodles

I am an inveterate doodler. I love to draw with a pencil and, in this book, you will find many of my little doodles. In addition, since this is a book about creating, I have left space throughout the book for you to create your own doodles along with mine. These fun shapes may eventually find their way onto your quilts. Save all your doodles, everything you think might have possibilities.

For doodling, I happen to love the Paper Mate® Sharpwriter® #2 pencil. It is a yellow plastic disposable mechanical pencil with an exposed eraser on the end, and looks just like a regular pencil. The soft lead is great and I love the eraser. It can be found at office supply stores. You no doubt will find your favorite as well.

You may even doodle while you are on the telephone. My daughter, Sarah, told me, “Every time you pick up the phone, Mom, you pick up a pencil and you doodle, and I bet you don’t realize you are doing it.” She is right; I doodle my way through napkins, tablecloths, phone books, address books, envelopes, and reams of scrap paper. If there is no paper, I write on my hand!

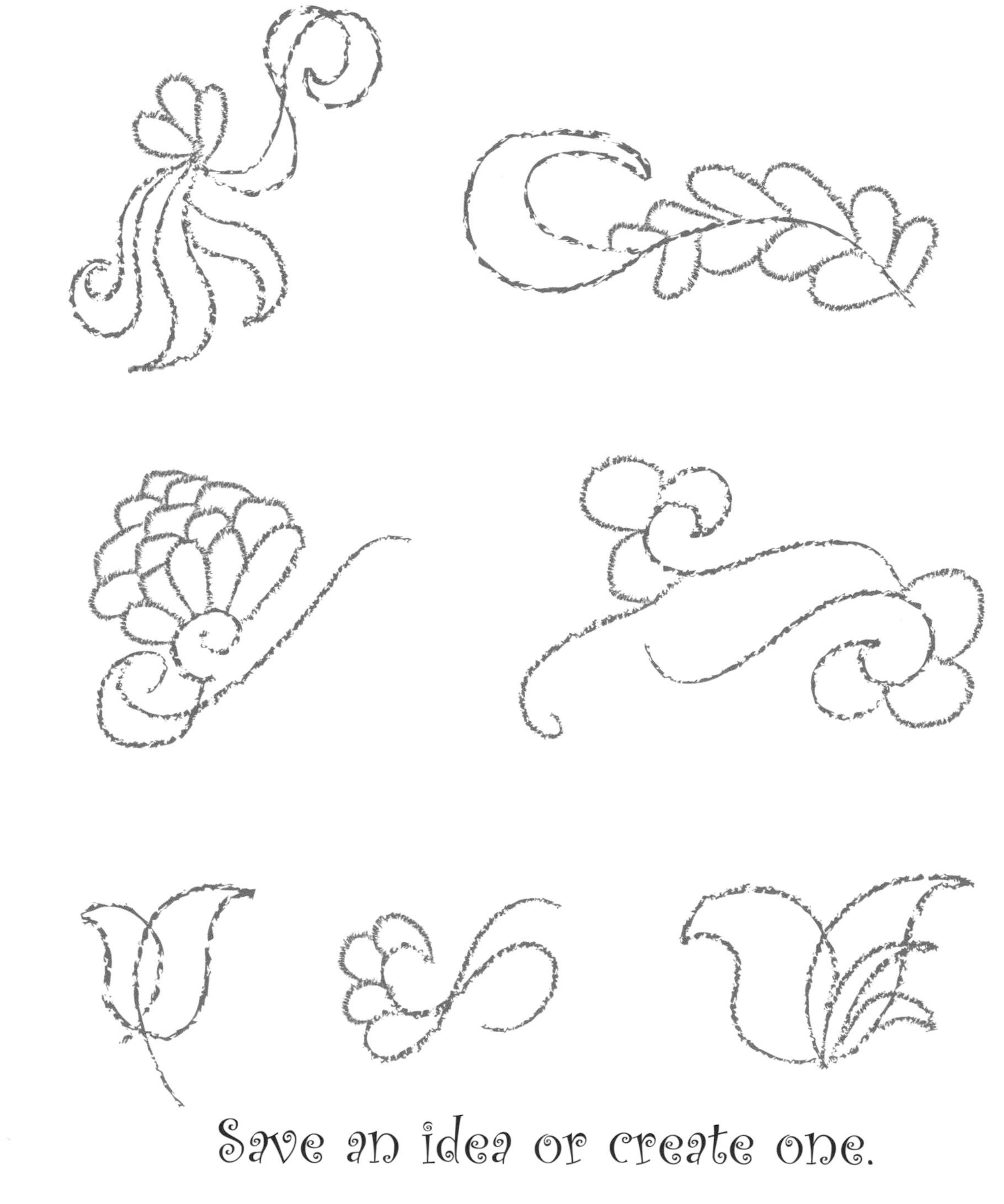

Organizing Designs & Doodles

Notebooks, along with a huge three-hole punch, are my best source for storing designs. They are on a shelf just above my cutting mat for easy access. When they become a chore to find, I will ignore them. If I rediscover them I am amazed at how exciting they are and why I kept them in the first place.

Next, I categorize the designs: *Victorian, Traditional, Early American, Oriental, Contemporary, Geometric, Whimsical.* From there, I will divide designs even further into blocks and border designs. Also, I'll place a small three-hole punched clear pouch at the front of the notebook to hold the smaller bits and pieces of ideas.

Then comes the mastery of the scanner and the technique of turning a design into a continuous line. There are many books and classes offered. I would certainly recommend taking a class on designing and design drafting. It is also worth taking time to learn how to use a scanner and printer. A flat-bed style scanner is easier to use than an upright printer/feeder style.

Of course, you can always use the local copy center or office supply store. When you use a copy service, take a Quilter's Assistant Proportional Scale (see Resources, page 93) to find the correct enlargement or reduction percentage. Some copy centers charge a dollar for doing the math and resizing the design for you. Save your dollar for buying another pattern or stencil.

Developing Cell Memory

When you practice the correct way to draw shapes and free-hand pencil quilt on paper, your brain does not know whether you are drawing patterns on paper or stitching the patterns at your machine. Yet, it understands the hand-eye coordination that increases as you practice the shapes, and you develop what I call *cell memory*. In addition, when you sit up straight, with your work directly in front of you, your hand-eye coordination increases even more. The most incredible thing to me is that this step-by-step system works exactly the same for a traditional sewing machine, shortarm system, midarm, or longarm machine.

Here is a good example of cell memory at work. My college age son, Justin, wanted to learn to play golf with Grandpa's clubs. We took him to an indoor golf facility to practice his swing. Each time he swung the clubs, it was as if he were swinging a baseball bat. All the time he had played baseball, from T-ball through Little League, he developed his cell memory to swing that golf club, not like a golf club, but like a baseball bat. He still loves the game of golf, but he took up tennis where the swing is more similar to baseball than golf. Cell memory at work. He is an excellent, tournament-winning tennis player, a natural, and now enjoys coaching younger tennis players.

It is the same with us; we draw hearts, we stitch hearts, and after a while it is like second nature. Sideways hearts, upside down hearts, big hearts, and small hearts are all stitched with ease using cell memory. When you start stitching as a beginner, and you are inconsistent, be *consistently inconsistent*.

If a shape is beautiful there is no "unstitching."

Practice doodling the shapes on paper to create cell memory and hand-eye coordination.

The Five Shapes of Quilting

There are five shapes in Sally Terry's Language of Quilting. They are the arc (or C-curve), the S-curve, the straight line, the loop, and the hook. You will find these shapes in almost every quilting pattern, whether it is a stencil, a printed pattern, or a pantograph. Combined, they form thousands of patterns.

You will notice that all the shapes curve except the straight line. This distinction will become important later as you discover how straight lines complement the other four shapes.

As you develop your cell memory by practicing the five shapes, you will learn that the first pathway gives you the freedom to create and execute any quilting motif.

Read the pattern

As you break down quilting patterns into the five individual shapes, you must find the beginning point and the ending point of each shape, as shown on page 13. I call this reading the pattern.

Look at wallpaper, paper towels, logos, and appliqué patterns, and you will see the five shapes. Notice where one shape ends and the next starts. Since you are now aware of the shapes, they will be easy to discern.

Practice hand-eye coordination

I often hear instructors say, "Practice, practice, practice." Yet, what do you practice when you are just starting out? Often there is nothing definitive given to us and we are on our own. Now, when you "practice, practice, practice" using the *Language of Quilting's* five shapes, you develop the cell memory and hand-eye coordination you need to execute any quilting design.

While we are doodling, we create something called cell memory. It gets your brain accustomed to making your hand travel in a certain path. Since your brain does not know if you are at your machine sewing a pattern or doodling the pattern on paper, it does not matter how you practice, just practice. Your brain simply cannot tell the difference.

Hand-eye coordination will not happen without practice. It will just happen a lot faster with this practice technique. Feel encouraged that you will not be "heart or leaf challenged" ever again.

Train eyes to focus ahead

To complete a shape you will focus ahead, rather than where you are quilting or where you were. Often times, your focus will be two to three inches ahead of the needle. Before you start moving the needle, or fabric to the needle for traditional machines, focus your eye ahead to the beginning point of the next shape. Then, when your needle or stylus gets to that point, you must immediately focus on the beginning point of the next shape, whether it is an arc, an S-curve, a straight line, a loop, or a hook. This is what I call *reading the pattern in motion.*

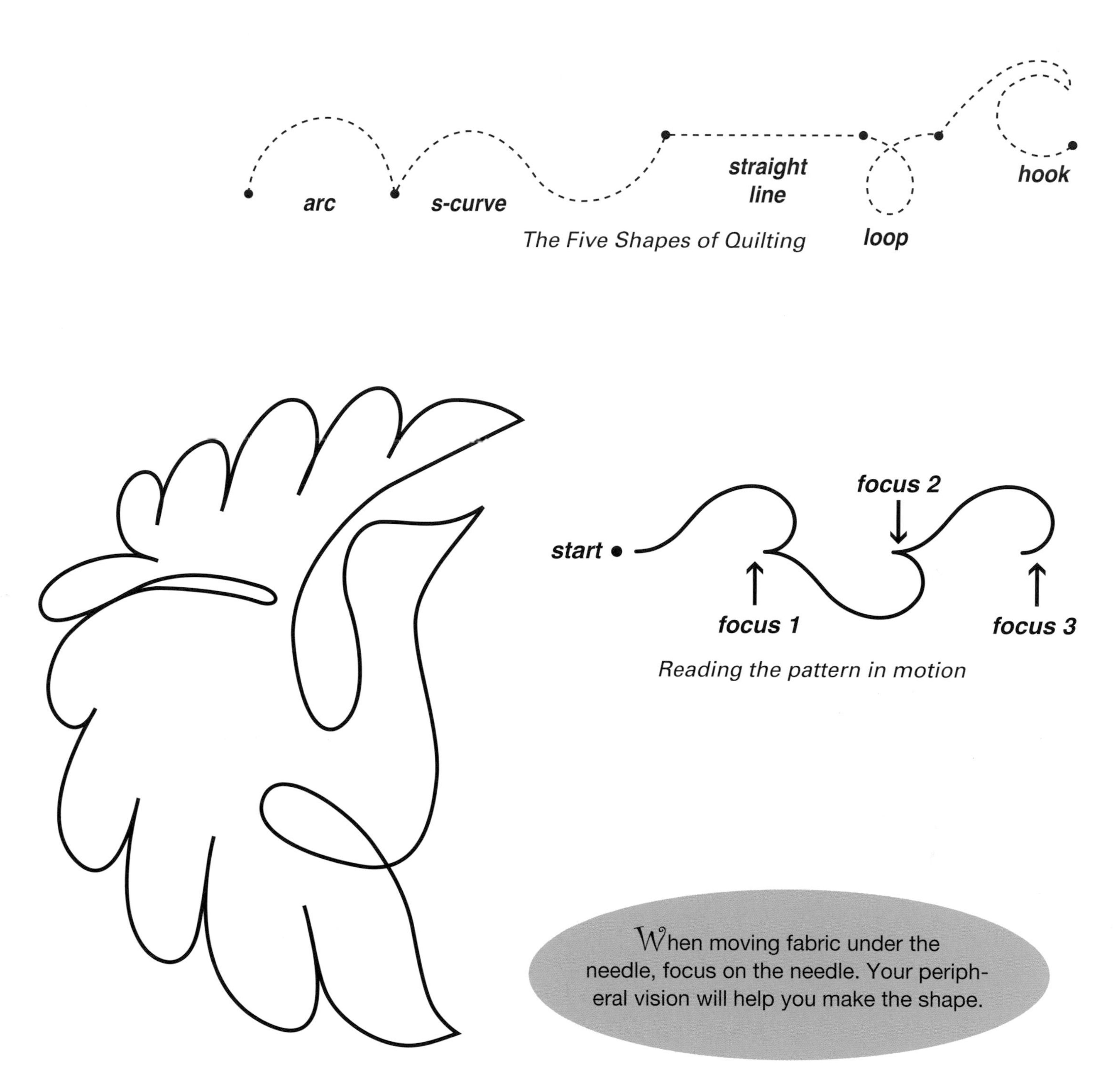

The Five Shapes of Quilting

Reading the pattern in motion

When moving fabric under the needle, focus on the needle. Your peripheral vision will help you make the shape.

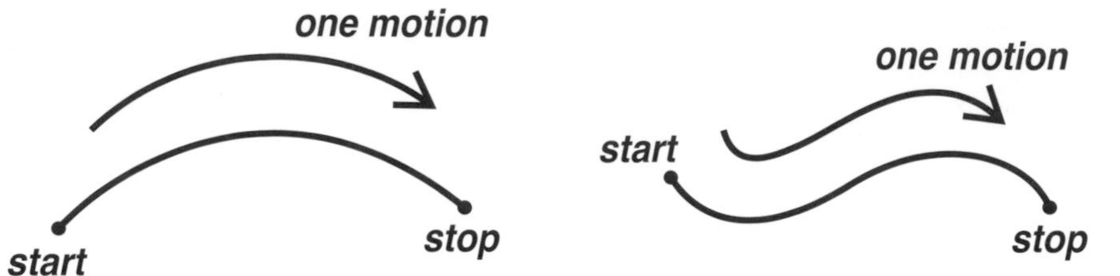

This is my signature sashing and border design. I offer it freely for you to use.

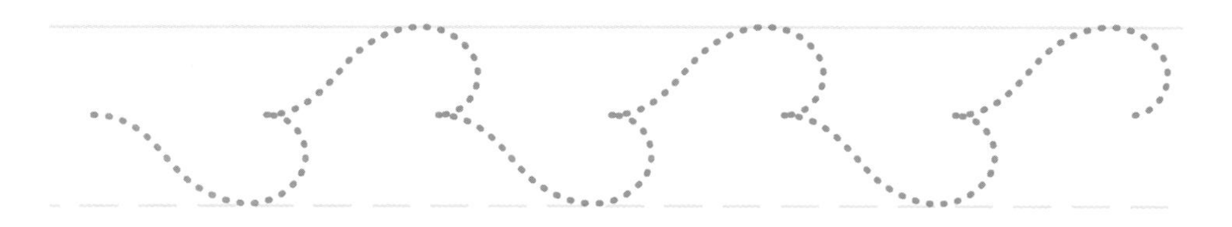

Develop smooth strokes

This is probably the most important technique I will share with you.

After you separate the patterns into individual shapes, execute each shape in one single movement. Each arc is one stroke; each loop is one stroke. All shapes are done with a single smooth stroke. Do not try to draw around the shapes; it's better to accomplish them with one stroke from where the shape starts to where it ends. Then stitch the next shape with a single stroke, and so on.

When your eyes focus on the proper area of the pattern, your hand will naturally follow your eye. To illustrate my point further, think about driving a car and having something on the side of the road catch your eye. Before you know it, you are heading in the direction you are looking (hopefully not off the road). Your hand follows your eye.

So, take advantage of this great gift of nature and focus ahead. Your patterns will be more accurate and you will be able to stitch hundreds of patterns you have passed up before. All it takes is enough practice to develop hand-eye coordination and cell memory of the five *Language of Quilting* shapes.

As you learn to focus ahead, remember to make all the shapes pretty. Even if the pattern is not quite what you hoped it would be, you may not have to unstitch an irregular attractive thread path.

Count for overall size consistency

Keep your hand movements smooth. With one stroke, draw each of the shapes and focus ahead. To help achieve consistency in the size of the shapes:

Count ONE for the **small** shapes.
Repeat one, one, one, drawing a complete shape with each count

Count ONE, TWO for the **medium** shapes.
Repeat one, two, one, two for each stroke of the medium shapes.

Count ONE, TWO, THREE for the **large** shapes.
Repeat one, two, three, one, two, three for each stroke of the large shapes.

Remarkably, this little counting trick helps you keep each shape consistent in size. Draw each shape enough times to feel the rhythm, until your consistency with each size improves.

Carry a notebook with you and, when you have an extra moment, fill the pages with the five shapes, counting to determine size. This is great practice when you are not at your machine.

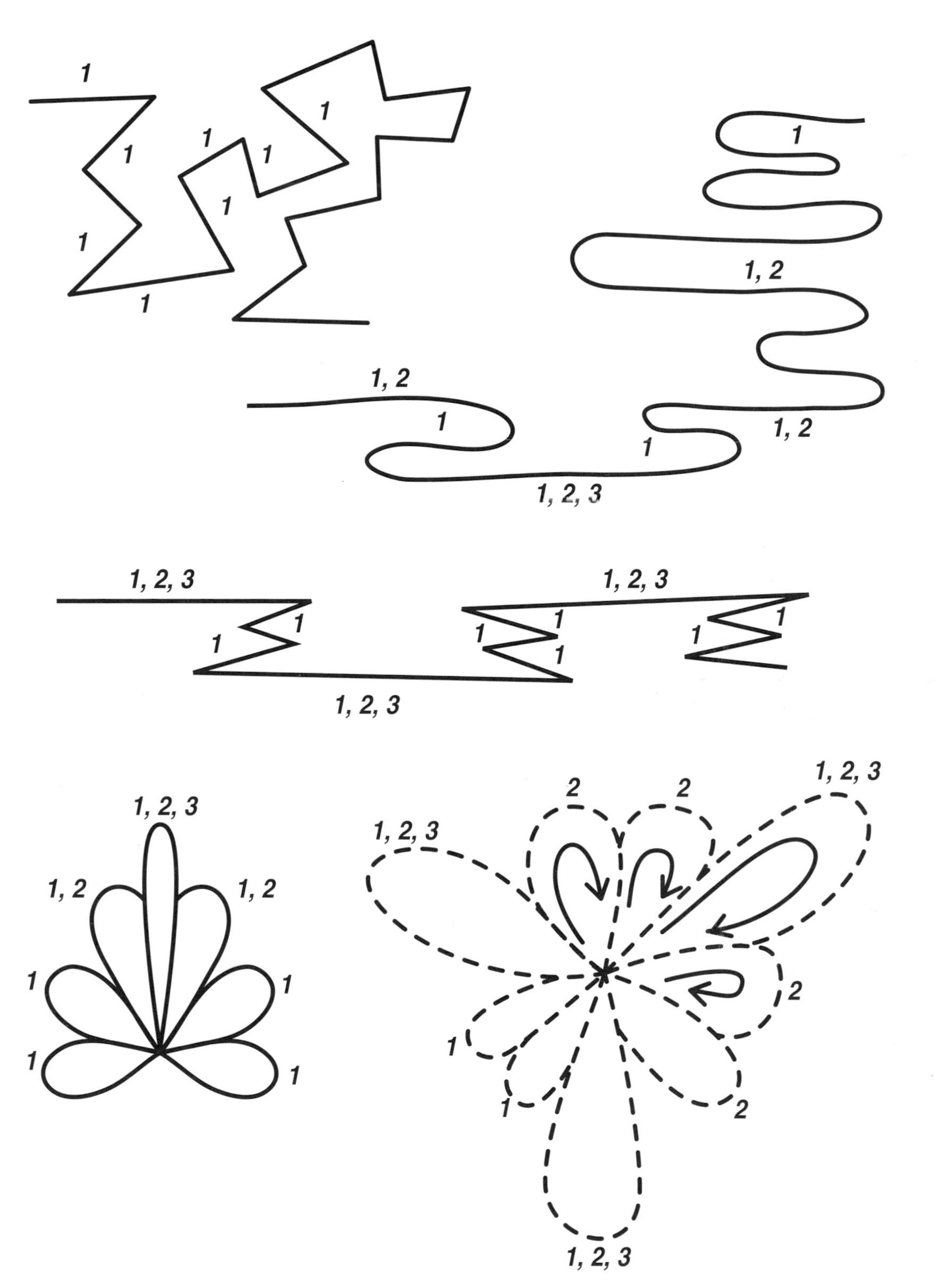

Feel comfortable drawing each shape in different sizes with consistency.

The Arc

The Arc or C-Curve, is a continuous curving line that curves in one direction. Trace the pattern with your finger. Find the smoothest continuous-line pathway without doubling back over lines. The wider arcs are smoother and easier to execute. Arcs also are easy to quilt because your wrist and elbows are the natural centers for making arcs.

To mark arcs on a country quilt, a woman would often hold a piece of chalk in her hand and place her elbow in the corner of the quilt top. As her arm swung around, the arc would appear.

The continuous-line pattern shown is made entirely of arcs. It starts with three small arcs, then it changes direction with one large arc to complete the pattern. You can repeat the pattern as many times as you need. Notice that when you rotate the pattern, it becomes a companion block pattern. Look closely to see the secondary circle-like pattern formed by careful placement of the original arc design.

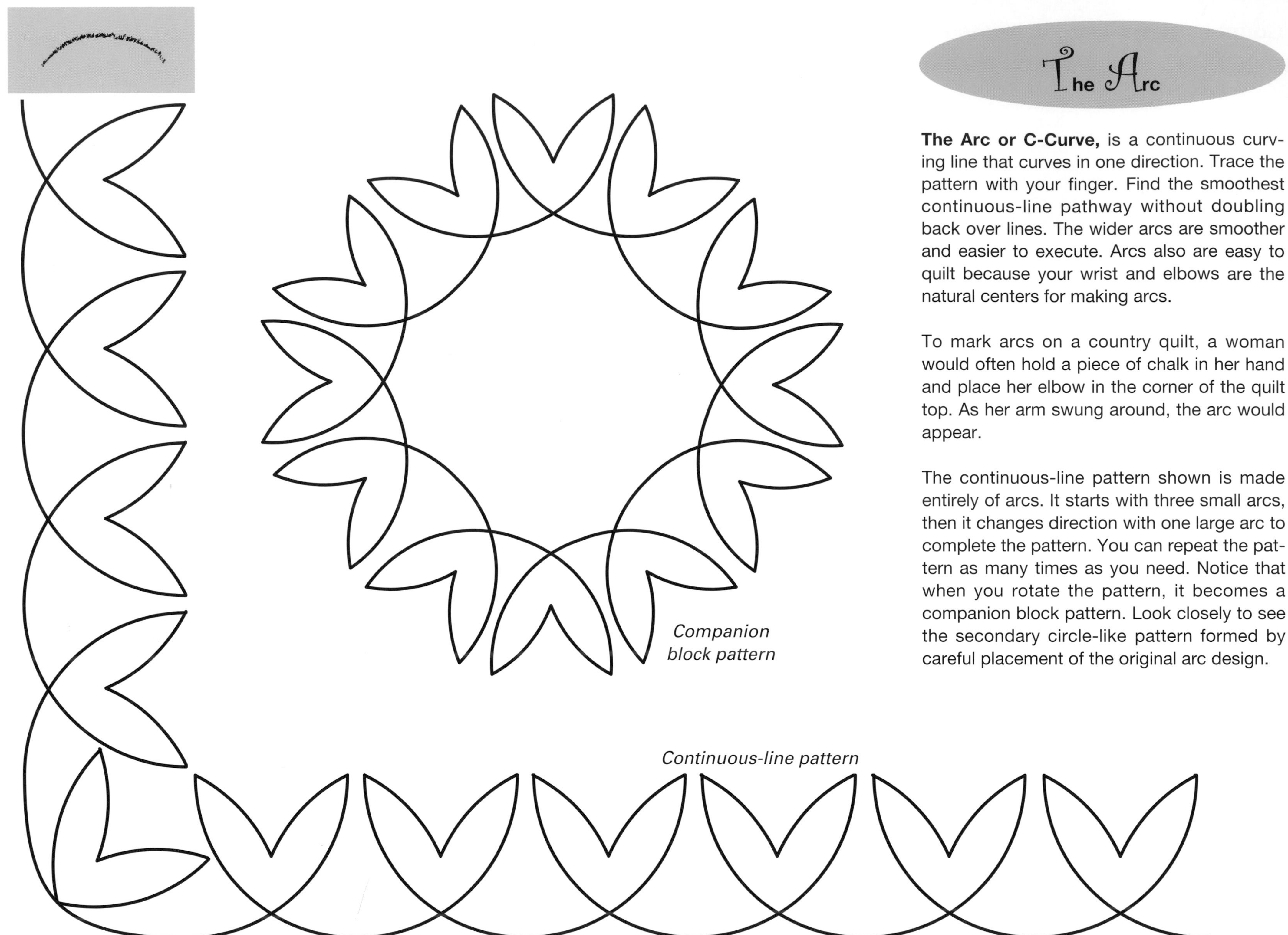

Companion block pattern

Continuous-line pattern

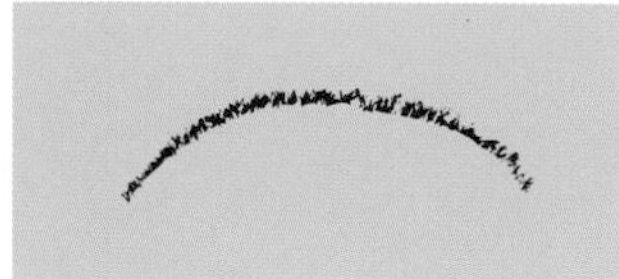

Arcs become *scallops* when traced around shapes. To make scallops, always aim for the center of the pattern. When quilting scallops around a circle or along a straight line, you must focus or your arcs will be different and will stretch out and lean to one side or the other.*

A *continuous arc* with a decreasing radius becomes a spiral. Just think of interstate entry and exit ramps when the curve just keeps getting tighter. A spiral works the same way. Think of a spiral as a series of arcs getting smaller and nesting inside one another as you stitch.

A series of arcs on their sides works well for fills, sashings, and borders. It is very important to keep the arcs a constant distance from each other and a consistent shape.

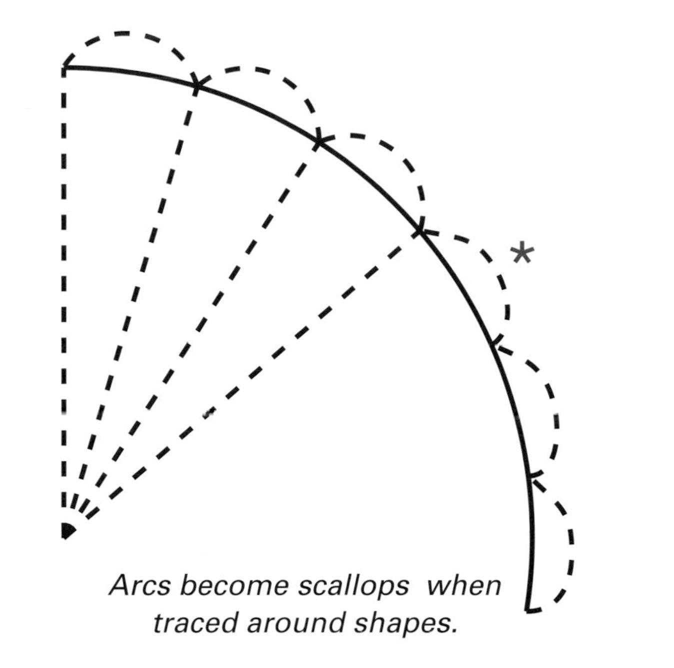

Arcs become scallops when traced around shapes.

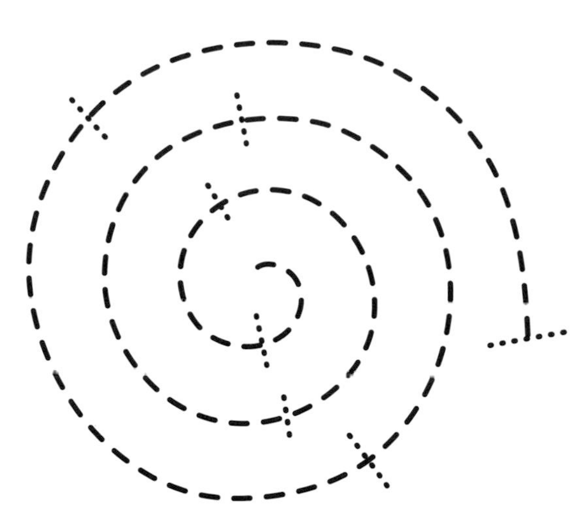

A continuous arc with a decreasing radius becomes a spiral.

When standing at a machine and quilting a spiral, move your entire body to quilt the spiral, holding your arms stiff by your side. Rock on your toes. Your body is smart. When sitting down, try keeping your arms and wrists stiff and move your upper body to make the spiral.

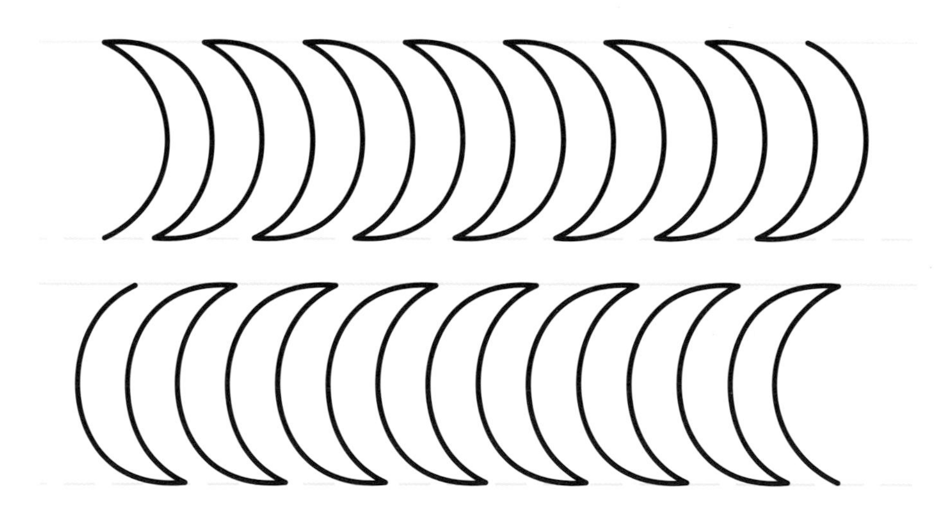

Fill, sashing, or border pattern made from arcs

Can you see the distinction between an Arc and an S-curve? These hearts are fatter and rounder, and they are made with arced lines that do not change direction. They are not S-curves. Trace these with your fingers to understand the movement and to feel the difference.

The S-curve is a continuously curving line that curves in more than one direction.

It is constantly rounded and curving. It is important to remember this when you are stitching a stippled or meandering pattern. In a stippled background pattern, the stitching lines are a series of S-curves that are less than ¼" apart. The lines in a meandered pattern are the same, but they are more than ¼" apart. Again, trace this pattern with your finger to feel the directions of the curves.

The heart border pattern below clearly shows the S-shape as it curves in two directions. Note the use of a pair of arcs to turn the corner in the border.* To make the hearts, stitch one series of S-curves as shown by the solid line, then bring the thread path back, using the same S-curves, but reversing them, as shown with the dotted line.

When I talk my way through an enclosed heart, I say "start top left bottom right." Start at the top, stitch the left side first in an S-shape down to the bottom of the heart, finish with a reverse S-shape up the right side back to the top and that will finish the heart. S-curve over and start another one.

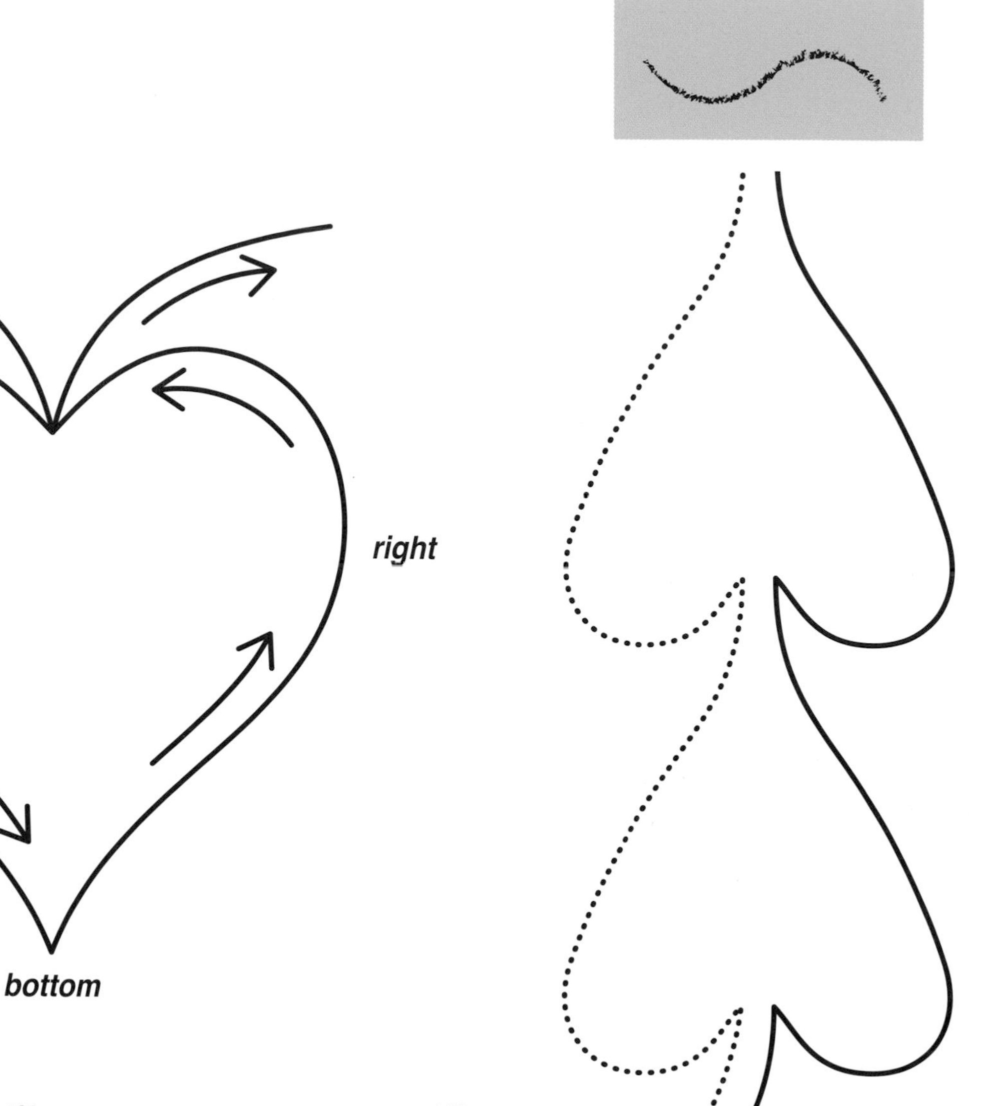

S-curve patterns that have a center line look great when stitched right down the center seam of a double border. The adjoining borders may be different sizes. Stitch each side of the border so the pattern will fill the area.

I am always leery of stitching a large border pattern over multiple borders, especially if the borders are made with contrasting colors. To complement both borders, consider using a variegated thread.

At left is a quick and easy way to do both borders at the same time, yet they appear as if they are treated separately. Besides, this way you do not have to stitch-in-the-ditch between the borders.

The trick here is to choose patterns and stencils that look terrific in many sizes, both big and small.

A series of S-curves on their side works the same way in sashing; again, consistency, size, and proportion are the most important factors in making them attractive.

Practice finger-tracing the patterns before you start stitching, or move the machine or fabric under the machinewithout turning it on. This is how you develop cell memory.

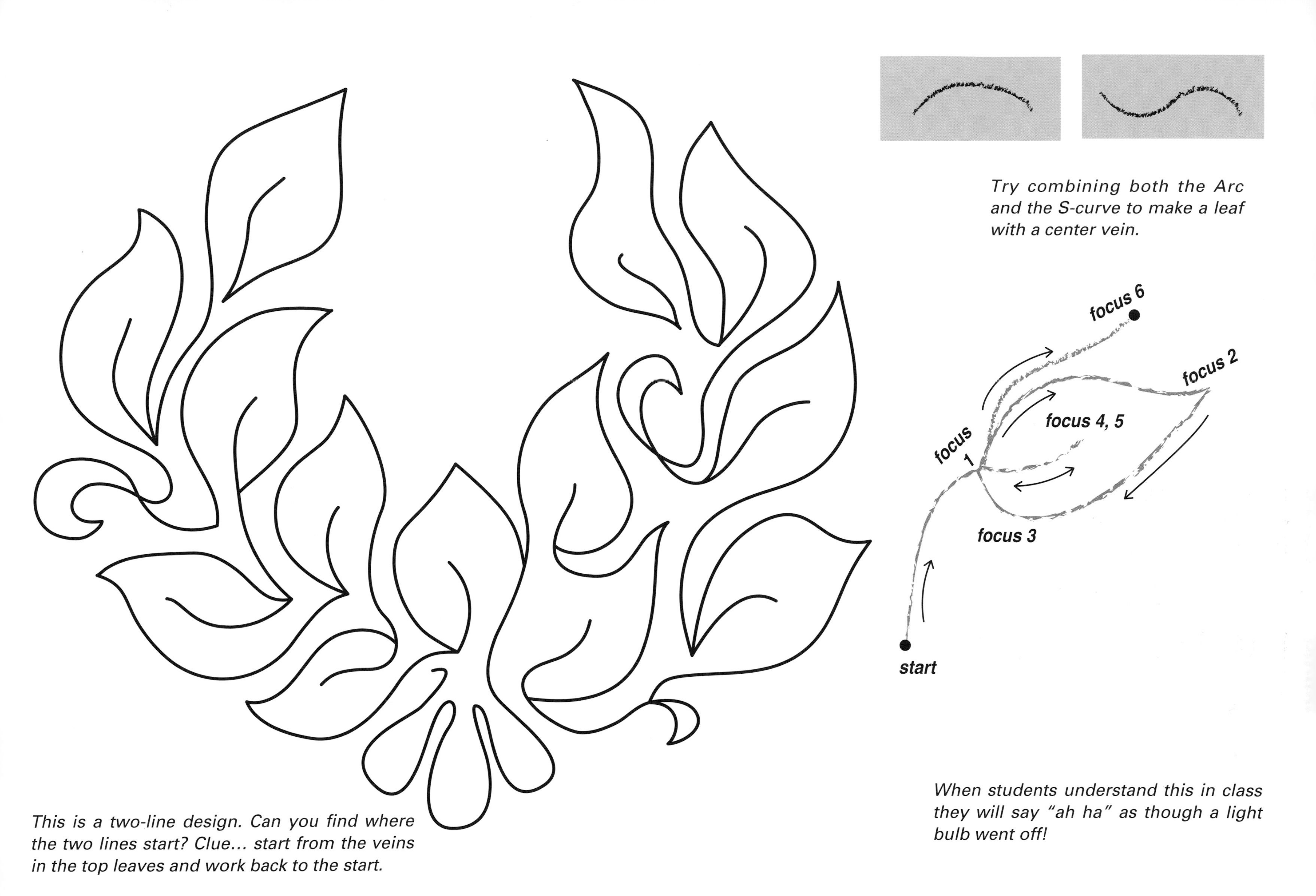

Try combining both the Arc and the S-curve to make a leaf with a center vein.

This is a two-line design. Can you find where the two lines start? Clue... start from the veins in the top leaves and work back to the start.

When students understand this in class they will say "ah ha" as though a light bulb went off!

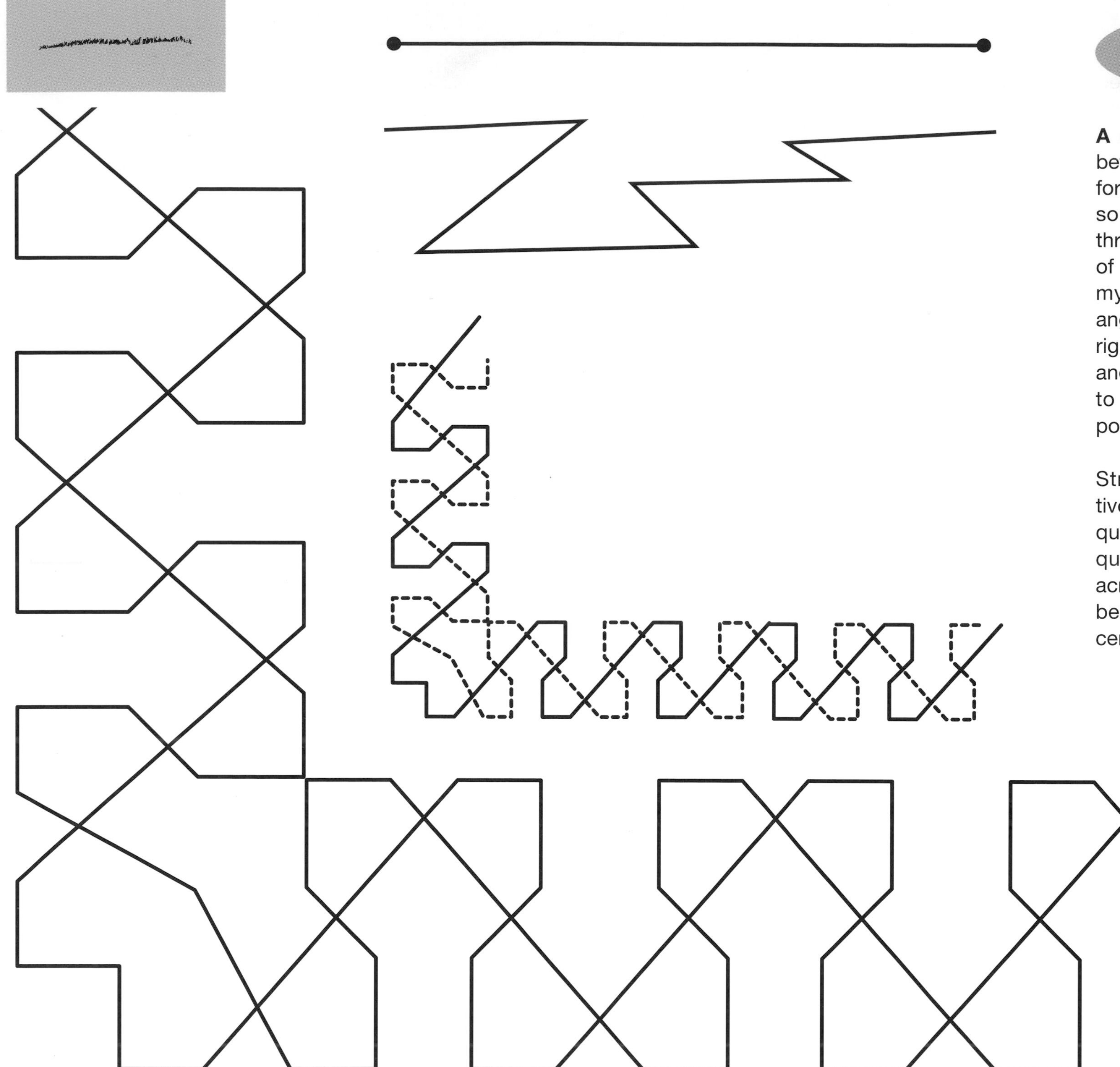

The Straight Line

A straight line is the shortest distance between two points. I am much more comfortable drawing curves than straight lines, so I have to concentrate and talk myself through the angle changes and line lengths of a straight-line fill pattern. When I talk to myself it sounds like this, "angle, angle, angle, angle." For a star "start up down left right." Practice making your lines straight, and your angles consistent. You may want to slow down a little when you get to a point to make a true sharp point.

Straight-line quilting patterns are effective on contemporary quilts and masculine quilts, and they look lovely behind appliqué. They add movement when stitched across a Nine-Patch block and they create beautiful texture in the large area around center medallions.

Straight parallel lines also work well when they contrast with the four basic curved shapes because they complement the curves. That is why you often see cross-hatching behind the graceful curves of an appliqué vine with flowers, or with the Sunbonnet Sue design.

The double-line border on page 22 is entirely made of straight lines. It also relates well to many pieced block patterns. Notice how the basic design looks when used with even spacing.

The single-line border design below is also made with only straight lines. The dramatic angles create movement and excitement. Imagine it on the border of a quilt for your favorite guy!

Quilt detail by Sally Terry

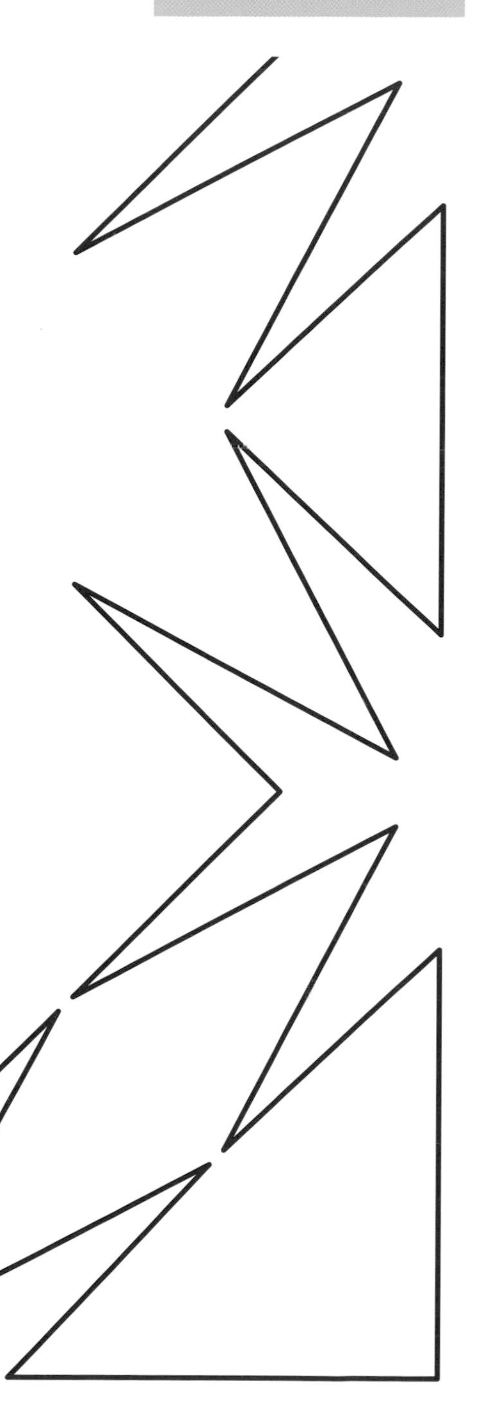

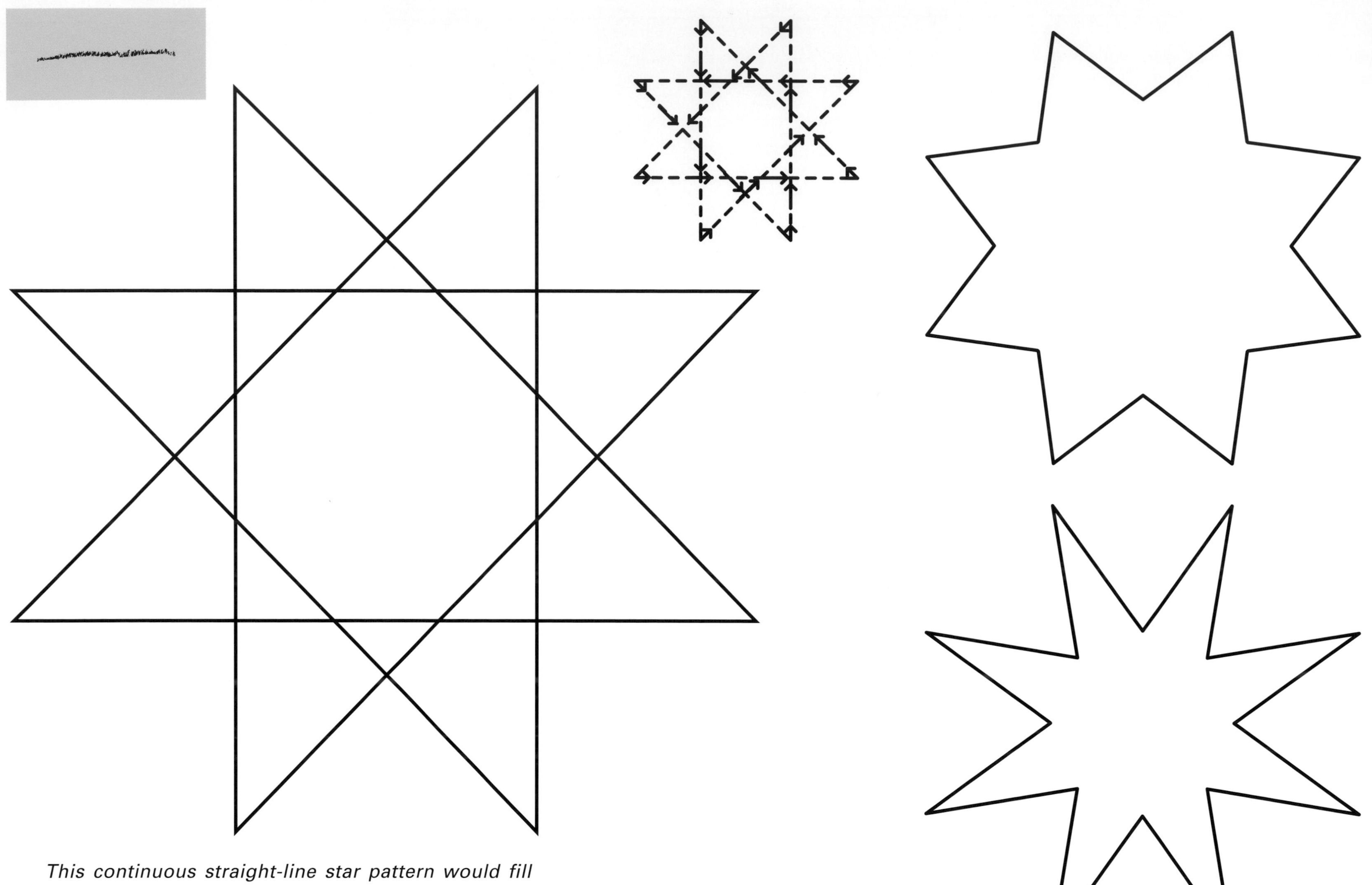

This continuous straight-line star pattern would fill any plain block effectively. You can use crosshatched lines, webbing, or curved lines to fill the center and complement the straight lines.

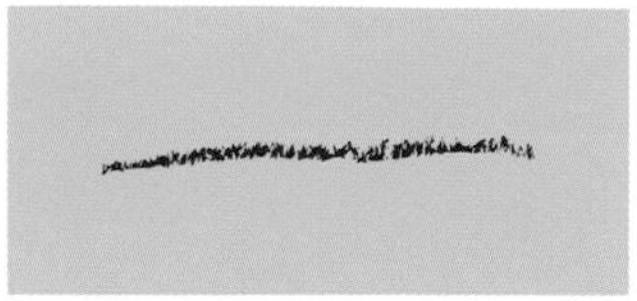

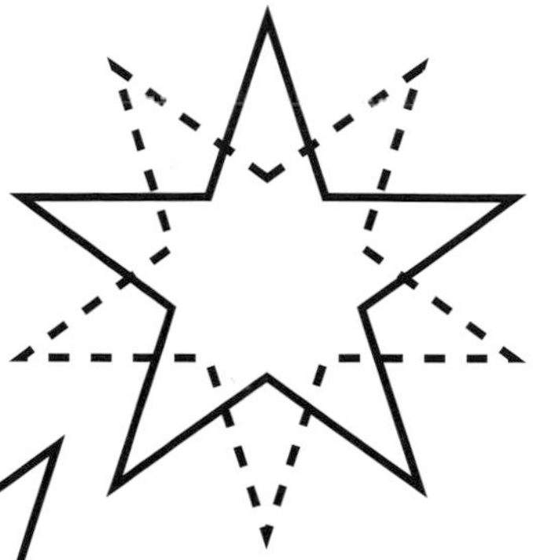

I call all straight-line and parallel-line patterns *freebies* (kind of like vegetables without butter when you are on a diet). Since they contrast so much with the curves, you can always add them to the mix.

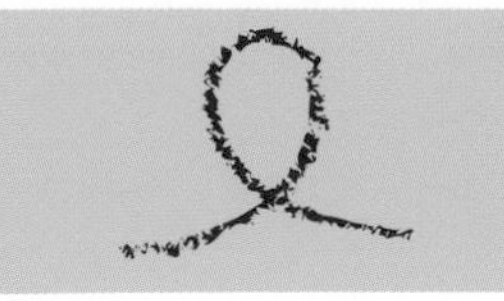

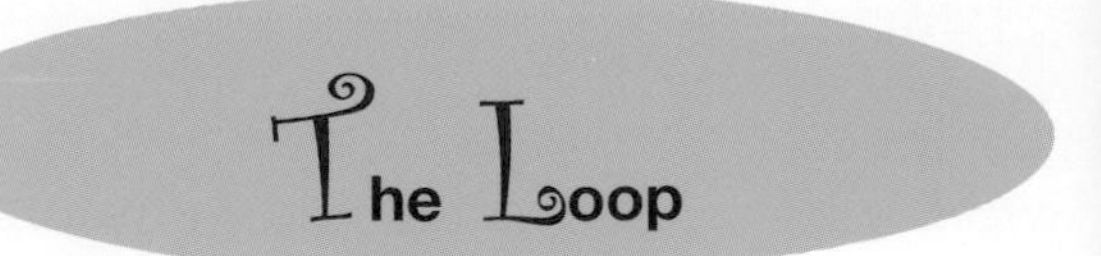

The Loop

The loop is a curve that crosses over or meets itself and encloses a space. Loops give you time to think when you are alternating between objects in a fill pattern. They combine well with any shape, such as stars, hearts, flowers, pumpkin seeds, and spoons. Used alone as a fill pattern, they look like beautiful eyelet lace.

The sweeping lines of loop patterns are easy to execute. When doubled, they become flower buds. Loops surrounding a shape give a delicate look, just as arcs or scallops. They can even fill other quilted shapes as they do in the hearts shown on the next page.

Loops combined with single-line S-curves work well in both small and large areas. Use these for sashings and borders, or for smaller areas where you just want to fill in a small space. It is best to close the open loop at each end of the design. Stitches not connected to other quilting will look better with your new start and stop arsenal.

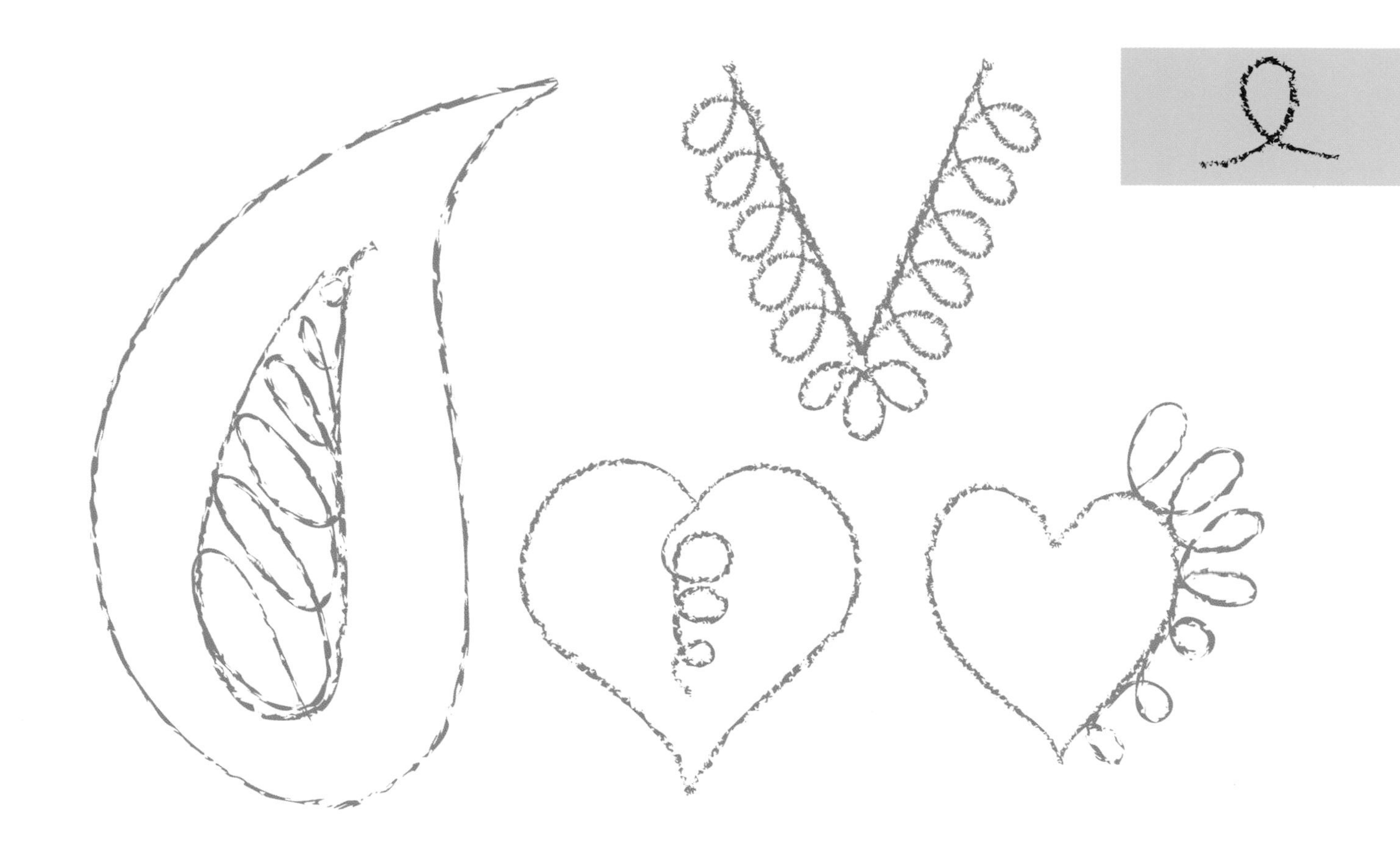

Loops should be in your arsenal of starts and stops.

Try doodling designs of your own.

To make a continuous-line pattern look truly continuous, start and stop the thread path in an inconspicuous area, such as a thread intersection, a point, or a corner. It is easy to tell where threads join on curves and in open areas of long thread paths. If you need to join threads on a curve or in an obvious place, it is better to unstitch the thread back to the last thread intersection and restart the pattern from there.

In this butterfly pattern you will find loops and arcs used together. Trace them with your finger, noting that the start is hidden where it will be easy to meet when the pattern is complete.*

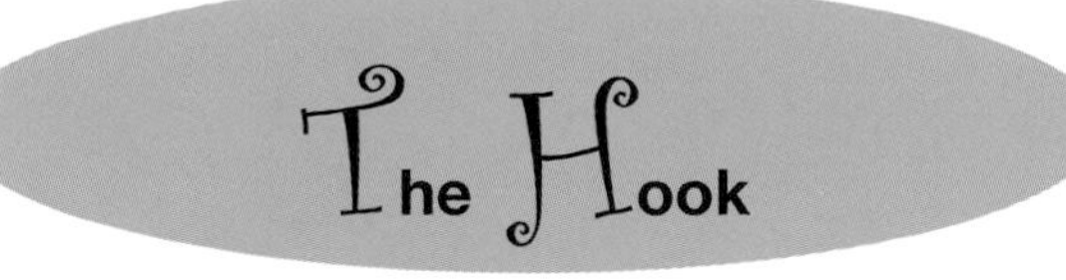

The Hook

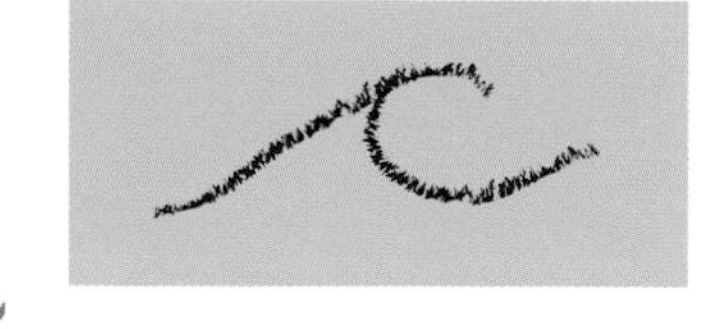

Multiple hooks look like waves in the ocean.

The hook consists of two arcs curled to a point; the point can be either open or closed, or the arcs can overlap each other. I always include the hook shape when I teach because it is easier to visualize than two arcs joined together.

You can use a series of hooks in a row as a fill pattern or in a border; they look like waves in the ocean. In the illustrations shown here, there are several different styles of hooks. I think that the deeper curls produce a better shape.

Stitched together, hooks can form all sorts of fanciful shapes that you can quilt in small or large plain squares, over block designs, or combined in sashing and borders.

You will find hooks at the center of roses and spirals. Hooks are the pathways of the wind, or ribbons, or curls surrounding a feathered heart. Hooks are usually asymmetrical, making them easier for a beginning machine quilter to accomplish. It's much easier to stitch paths that don't have to match exactly.

Asymmetrical loops and hooks fit well into different shapes when used as a freehand pattern. Hooks are regal and decorative. Notice how they can add elegance and beauty to a simple leaf design on the following pages.

Two arcs are curled to a point, forming a hook.

They will burst forth like fireworks and fountains, as water spouting from a whale.

Doodles for hook designs

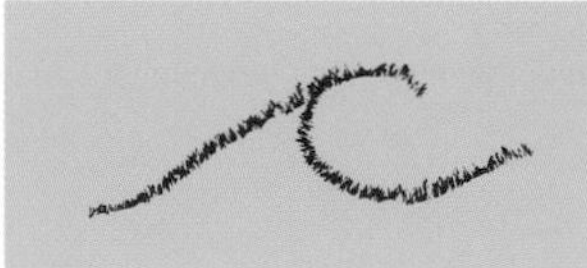

Hooks are regal and decorative. They add elegance and beauty to any leaf design.

Hooks are the pathways of the wind or ribbons and curls surrounding a feathered heart.

Patterns

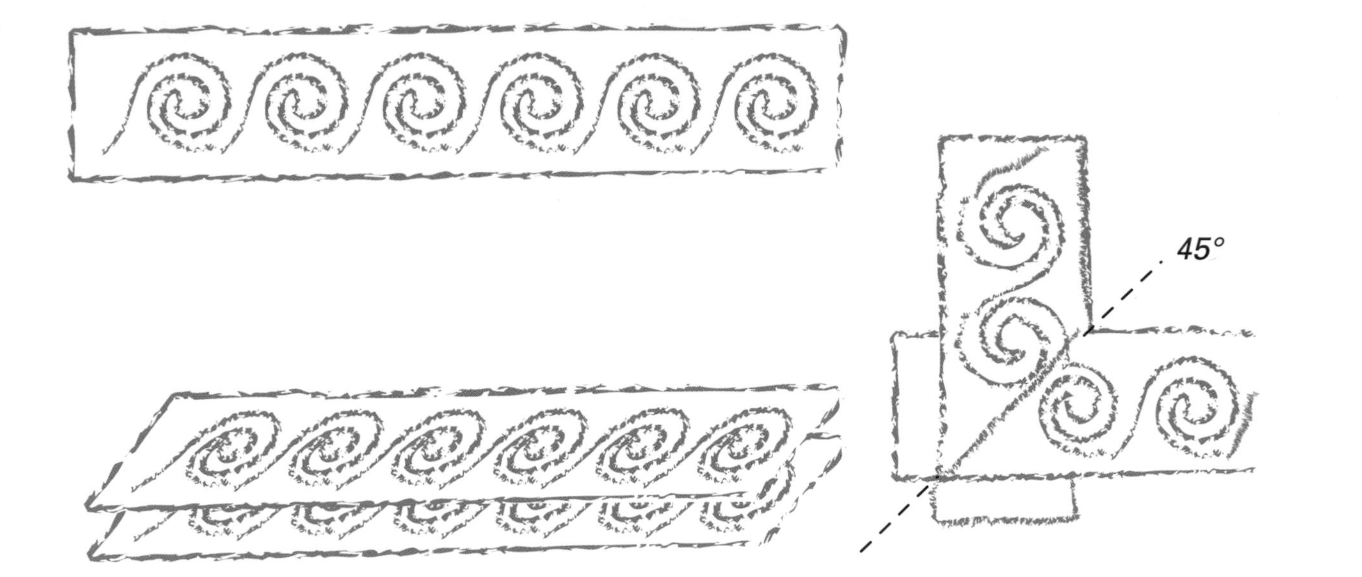

Multiple copies of the same pattern can be used to create corners and blocks.

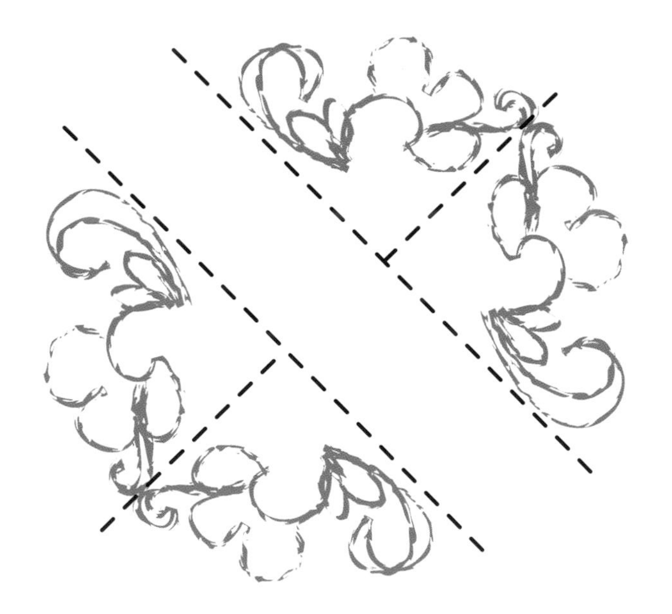

Making Corner and Block Patterns. Many patterns, especially those for borders, come with companion patterns for corners and blocks. It is a good idea to purchase these when they are available. Golden Threads makes pantographs called "Block and Roll."* Each roll pattern is approximately 12 feet long and includes both right- and left-corner patterns for border work, edge to edge patterns with interlocking guides, plus a complementary block pattern. It is easy for you to make them yourself, using a border design.

To make a corner pattern, trace or stitch the pattern onto two layers of thin paper. I recommend Golden Threads Quilting Paper.* Lay them one on top of the other, and holding them at one end, fold them apart to form a corner. When folded carefully, they will form a 45-degree angle. If you prefer, you can draw 45-degree lines on the patterns, then fold the paper on the lines and place them together. Try folding at different parts of the design for different corner patterns.

For longarm, midarm, and shortarm systems there are pre-printed pantograph grids available.*

To make a block pattern, use the corner pattern created from the border pattern to make a companion block pattern. Make two tracings of the corner pattern, then align them to form the block design. You may need to add or erase a few lines to make them more attractive or easier to sew.

* See Resources, page 93.

Selecting Patterns. Use the *Five Shapes of the Language of Quilting (pages 16-31)* as you start picking out patterns to use on the quilt top. Begin by looking at the designs shown here and breaking them into the five basic shapes. Place start and stop marks at the beginning and end of each shape.

Practice session – Using quilting paper, place the paper over the pattern and trace. Because the paper is so transparent, you can focus ahead to the end of the single shape and make one stroke with your pencil to complete the shape. Continue drawing/tracing until you have developed a rhythm and feel comfortable reading the shapes.

Quilting paper or tracing paper is transparent enough to see through, even when you use multiple layers. It is very strong and does not tear under your pencil. Marks are easy to erase. Moreover, it takes all the different mediums including chalk pencil, water-soluble markers, ink, pencil, and permanent markers.

Practice, Practice, Practice

Practice session – To stitch a cluster of leaves, start in the center and work your way around the cluster in either a clockwise or counterclockwise progression. When you are finished stitching, you will be back in the center where you started. In addition, the hook shapes provide a finishing touch for the design.

Can you feel the rhythm and are you counting?

hapes

Shapes in a Single Row. To become proficient in sewing shapes, it is important to practice. Prepare a worksheet by placing a piece of Golden Threads Quilting Paper or other translucent paper on your cutting mat. Following the ruled lines, draw a series of lines one inch apart, lengthwise. Draw as many lines as you can. Do this with several sheets of paper.

Practice Session – Draw a series of arcs along the first row; draw enough of them to feel the rhythm of the stitching. Challenge yourself to make them consistent by counting. Repeat with the S-curves, then the remaining shapes. Do many rows of each shape, making sure that you find the rhythm each time. Practice repeating the shapes in a row. This repetition would make perfect designs to use in sashing strips!

With another sheet marked in one-inch rows, practice drawing the five shapes again, this time drawing them in increasingly larger scale.

Another thing to consider is that you might be better at drawing or stitching shapes in one direction or the other. It might be that you are right- or left-handed, or straight-line or curved-line minded, or right-feathered, or left-hearted. I struggle to make straight-line fill patterns balanced and consistent in shape. Yet, I have no problem with curved fills and patterns. You may find the same thing.

Practice Session – Put the paper in your traditional sewing machine and practice by needle punching over your lines without threading your needle. Count and focus, be smooth and consistent – use the pathways!

Shapes in an Irregular Area. When you practice fill patterns and meandering, outline the outer boundary of the shape first, whether it is a square, a circle, a triangle, or even an irregular shape. Defining the space first will force you to think ahead so you do not box yourself into a corner.

Practice Session – Fold several 8½" x 11" sheets of paper as shown. On one sheet, fill each area with one of the five shapes. Vary the size and the angles, drawing the shape in one continuous line.

Remember to keep your eyes focused on where you want your pencil to go, rather than on the line you are drawing. Your pencil will touch that point more times than not. As you continue to practice, focus ahead. Fill the spaces evenly with the five shapes, using one continuous line. When you are inconsistent, be *consistently inconsistent*.

Vary the shapes, angles, and sizes until you have control. When you are inconsistent, you can make it look consistent or planned by varying the size, shape, and angle of the shapes. Take care to keep the distance separating the stitching lines, as well as the stitch length, consistent. A large part of the beauty of patterns is the consistency of the space between the stitching lines.

Remember that you are developing cell memory. As your skills advance, your shapes will become more stylized, and they will become individual to you.

Practice Session – Fold a piece of paper as shown. Place dots on the fold lines approximately an inch apart. Choose one of the five shapes and practice drawing it from dot to dot, graduating sizes as you practice down the page. Continue this practice until you feel comfortable drawing all five shapes at all angles and in all sizes. Focus ahead.

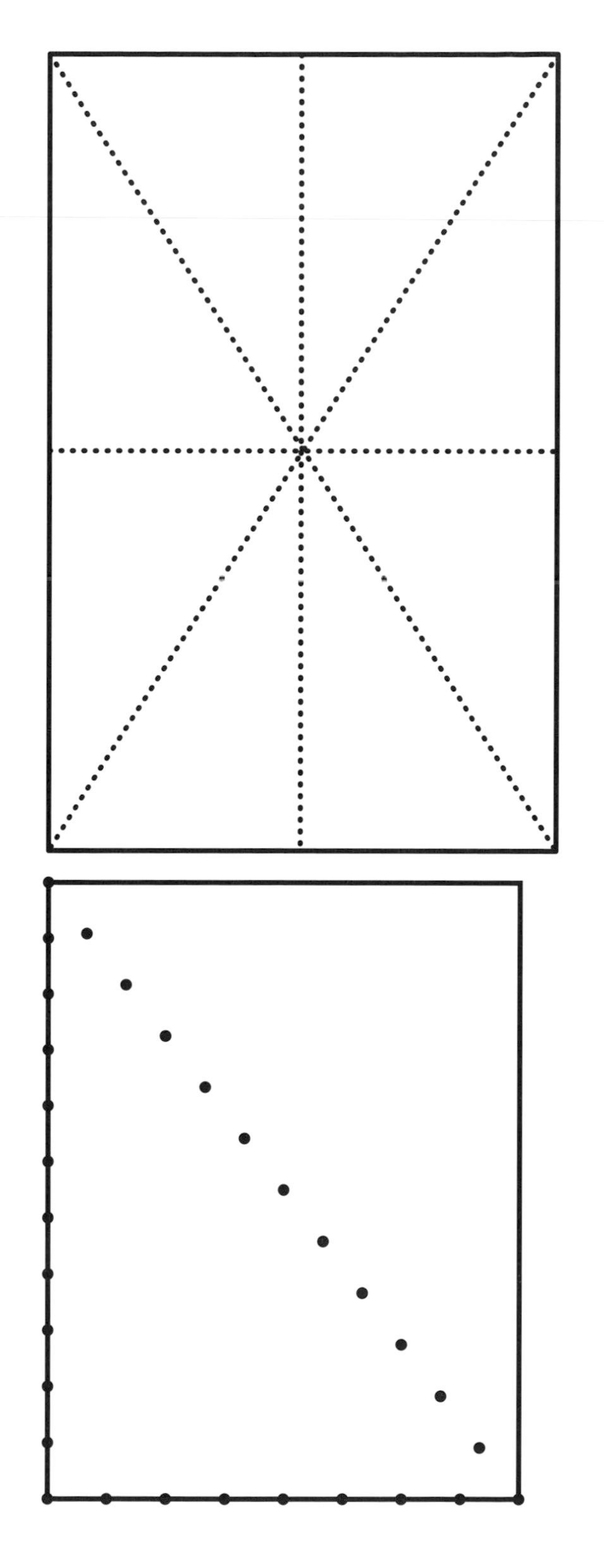

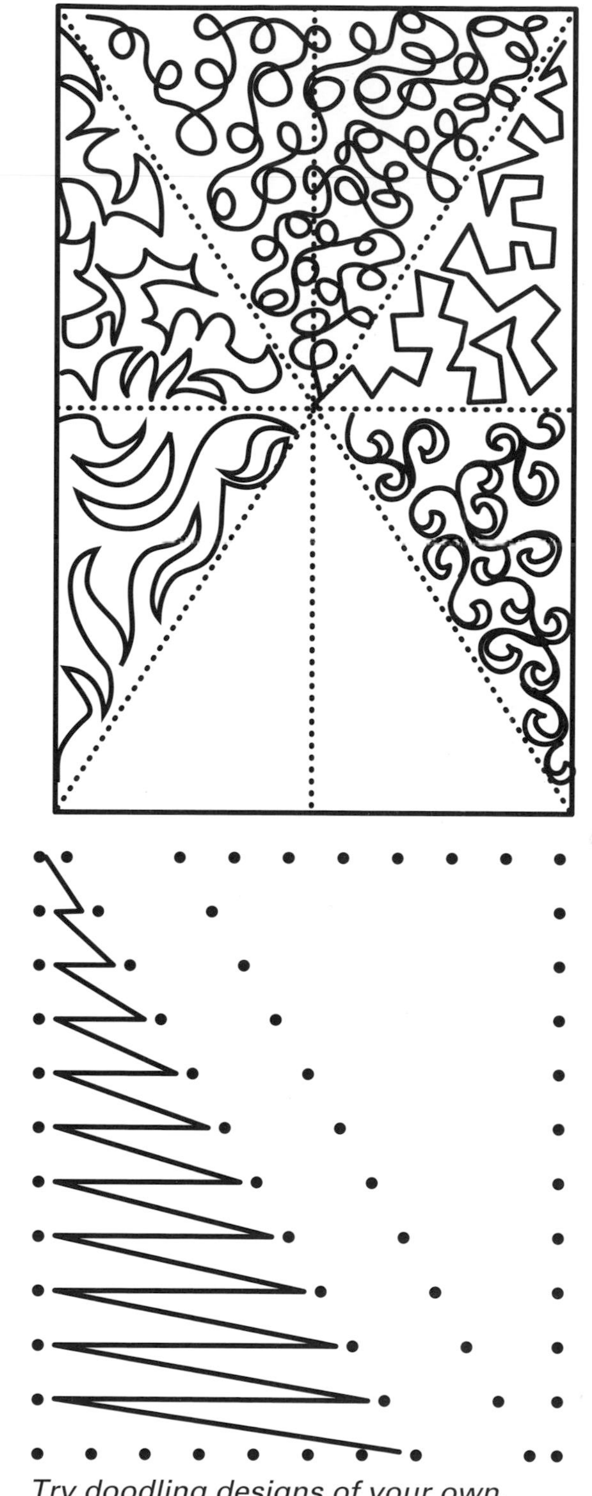

Try doodling designs of your own.

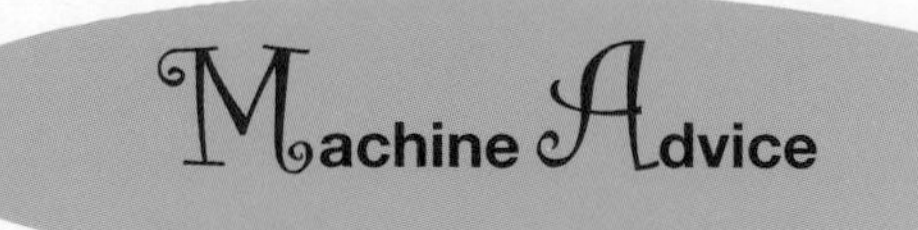

Working at the Machine. If you have been doing all the practice sessions, you have practiced a lot with a pencil. Now it is time to go to the machine. You do not have to use thread, but it's a good idea to get the feel of quilting these shapes while the needle moves up and down.

Before you start sewing, make sure your machine is set up properly. Traditional machines that have a bobbin sensor will need to have a bobbin in the bobbin case. It can be full or empty, but if it's full, don't thread the bobbin. To bypass the effect of a top thread sensor, insert a business card in the tension slot. Check your manual for more information or check with your local dealer. If you are using a longarm machine, remove the bobbin case, and load a small practice muslin sandwich.

I prefer to do a freehand stitch on a traditional machine with the feed dogs up because I feel I have more control. Try it both ways and see what you think.

Secure one sheet of your drawings from an earlier practice to a muslin sandwich with quilting adhesive spray or pins. Use an unthreaded needle to trace your pencil lines. Follow the stokes, focusing ahead, and use smooth, continuous strokes to complete each of the shapes.

Practice Session – Fold another sheet of quilting or tracing paper corner to corner and side to side as you did before, and place a series of dots on the fold lines. This time, stitch the designs from dot to dot without the pencil lines. Try to make the needle-punched shapes the same as the penciled ones, paying attention to stroke counts and rhythm.

Some shapes will go fast, and some will go more slowly. Remember to focus on where you are going, not where you are or where you have been. Use a single stroke for each shape, counting from one to three for the different sizes, and develop a rhythm.

Pathways to Choosing Quilting Designs

The most frequently asked questions in my quilting classes are –

How do you come up with pattern ideas to stitch into the quilt top?
Can you help me visualize the quilting patterns on the finished quilt?

Here are the answers to these questions in an easy to follow format. You have the talent and ability and I want to help you find it. Don't be afraid of your intuition. Just the fact that you chose this book means that you are ready to make creative decisions.

Utilizing Your Creative Sense

Collect some of the continuous-line quilting patterns you have on your shelf. Look for the beginning and ending of the combinations of arc, S-curve, straight line, loop, and hook patterns. Trace the patterns with your finger.

Practice Session – Group your patterns by the most obvious of the five basic shapes. You can group and divide further by the second most obvious of the five shapes you desire.

Notice how compatible they are in each group.

Practice Session – Choose your favorite sets. We are starting to use our creative sense to combine quilting design shapes that will be compatible together and which we can use on tops.

Compare your doodle patterns with the patterns you have chosen here, and notice where their similarities lie.

Practice Session – Look at the two groups of examples shown here. The first group has arcs and S-curves that come together to form points, giving all the patterns a similar feel. The second group has arcs that form feather or heart shapes, making them compatible with one another.

Combining the 5 Shapes With Your Creative Sense

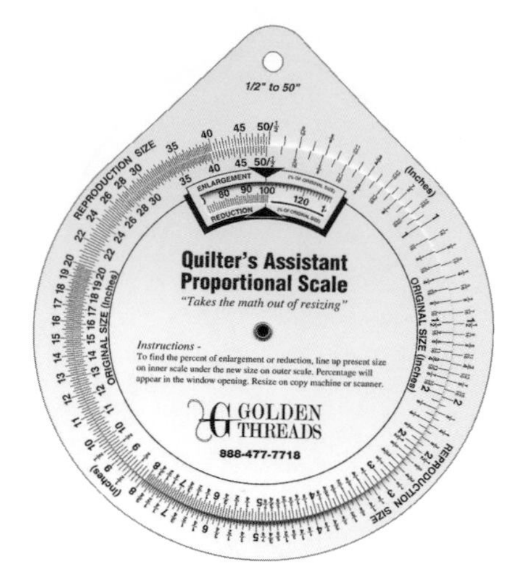

Resizing Quilting Motifs

Sometimes the pattern you need is not available in a size that is appropriate for the quilt. It's easy to change the size of patterns using a scanner or copier. To make sure that you get a copy that is the size you need, use the **Quilter's Assistant Proportional Scale** (Resources, page 93). It takes the math out of resizing appliqué shapes. The Proportional Scale or QAPRO is an invaluable tool as you can also use it to resize piecing patterns.

There is an outer scale, an inner scale, and a window on the QAPRO. The numbers are shown in fractions (1/4" rather than .25) making it easier when you are working in inches. With the QAPRO, you can determine how to enlarge or reduce the image proportionally on a copier or scanner.

- To resize a paper pattern using the QAPRO, measure one side of the area that you want to quilt, not including the unstitched margin area.
- Position and measure the chosen pattern in relationship to the area.
- To determine the percentage of enlargement or reduction, find the size of the printed pattern on the inner scale (wheel), then turn the wheel so the original size lines up with the new desired size on the outer scale. *The percentage of increase or decrease will appear in the window opening.*
- For example, if you have a 5" original image and you want to enlarge it to 7", find the 5" on the inner wheel, and turn the wheel so the 5" line is on the 7" mark on the outer scale. The percentage of increase indicated in the window is 140%. Copy the pattern at 140% to get the new correct size 7" pattern. Make multiple copies at 100% if needed.

Use a scanner to elongate or condense only one dimension and follow the printing instructions. If the scanner or copier cannot produce the amount required in one step, reduce or enlarge the image a second time. Measure the resized design and do the calculations again to determine your final measurements. This method is the most accurate to reach your desired size.

Use a calculator. Use a calculator to determine the scale by dividing the desired measurement by the actual measurement to find the scale factor. Multiply the scale factor by 100 to arrive at a percentage, since a photocopier increases and decreases by percentages. This works for both increasing and decreasing the pattern size.

Use either the greatest length or width of the original pattern, whichever dimension is easier to measure with the most accuracy. Lay the pattern on your cutting mat for the best accuracy.

1½" wide 75%

2" wide 100%

original size

3" wide 150%

4" wide 200%

Before Transferring Patterns

Keep the size of the unquilted margin, block, sashing or border in relation to the size of the quilt, whether it's baby-, wall-, or king-sized. A good rule of thumb for the average quilt is to leave an even margin on each side of the quilting pattern. Remember to leave an additional ½" on the outside of the border for the binding seam. Consider unquilted block margins in relation to the size of the quilted motif as well.

Use extra layers to create multiple repeat patterns using the needle-punched method. You can create up to fifteen layers of needle-punched patterns at a time with Golden Threads Quilting paper. The perforated holes from the needle feel like braille and can be placed face up and used with a pouncer pad for hard to see fabrics.

I always finger trace patterns before I quilt them, especially if the thread path is not obvious to me. I will also finger trace patterns I am familiar with but have not used in a while. If you always practice by finger tracing the pattern or by moving the fabric under the needle without the machine running, you will have smooth, professional-looking shapes that will not have to be unstitched. Doing this refreshes your cell memory. I will also mark the thread pathway on the stencil itself and lay it next to my pattern to follow.

Keep the original needle-punched layer. You can use it to make more patterns for other quilts.

Remember, if you pull your quilt gently on the bias, the paper will pop away from the stitches and is easily removed with a vacuum cleaner hose. Or just pull it away by tearing against the stitches. It will tear away clean eliminating the need for tweezers and a magnifier glass.

Always test your marker on the fabric before marking the entire quilt.

No-Marking Method
by Golden Threads

Select a continuous-line quilting design. Resize the design on a copy machine to fit the project. TRACE the design on paper.

Stack several sheets together placing the traced copy on top. Pin to secure and machine STITCH using a large unthreaded needle.

Separate the tear-away stencils. Pin to project and QUILT following the holes using free-motion quilting methods.

TEAR the paper from quilted area. Golden Threads Quilting Paper removes cleanly and easily without pulling stitches.

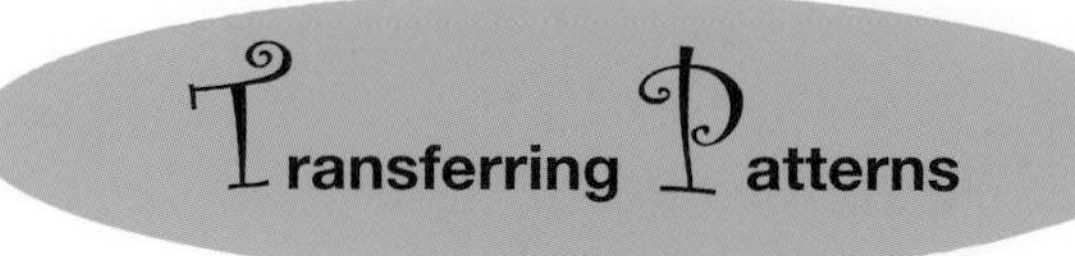

- You may prefer to use a light table to transfer your pattern. If you choose this method, you must mark the quilt *before* you baste it into a sandwich or load it into the frame of the longarm machine.

- If you are using stencils, scrub powdered tailor's chalk into the stencil lines. Use a hook-and-loop-type clothes brush to remove the excess chalk after the quilting is complete. You can also mark stencils with a washable chalk pencil or marker. Remove these marks after quilting. When water-soluble or air-soluble markers are used, it is recommended to rinse the quilt twice, with water only, before using detergent or quilt soap.

- You can also trace the pattern with a permanent marker onto tulle or wedding-veil netting. To transfer the design from the tulle to the quilt, trace over the tulle with a removable chalk pencil or marker. Look for tulle with small holes and minimum stretch.

Practice Session – Unroll some Golden Threads Quilting Paper over the area to be quilted, and trace the important lines. On the tracing, mark off the margin area between the design and the border. This margin is not quilted.

Fold three layers of the quilting paper large enough to cover the complete design area and cut it off the roll. Sketch or trace your pattern choices on the folded layers, one design to a layer, using a washable pencil or removable marker. Do *not* mark on the original top tracing.

Place the traced designs over the appropriate section of the quilt and evaluate your choices. When you are pleased with the design, transfer it to the original top tracing. To transfer the markings, use the No-Marking Method by Golden Threads as illustrated on the left.

Pin the paper in place on the quilt or use temporary spray adhesive, being sure to center the design. Then stitch, following the needle-punched lines or the tracing. It is important to know that the heat made by the action of the thread and needle can transfer permanent marker ink to the fabric. I prefer to use a marking method that is easy to remove from the quilt top fabric.

Fills, Stippling & Meandering

Fill Patterns. Use a fill pattern to make an area appear to *recede*, providing contrast that allows a featured motif to stand out. The fill pattern gives the area an even distribution of light and shade with a mottled effect. Fill patterns are repeating motifs that nest next to one another. Even though the pattern sequence usually stays the same, it may have various sizes and angles.

Fill patterns are closely stitched patterns. They are an essential part of the quilting design because they accent the area they surround. When you practice fill patterns, it is best to practice drawing them inside a defined space. Draw an irregular shape such as the shape you might find around an appliquéd area. Use your pencil to fill in the shape with a fill pattern. Try it again with another fill pattern, or with a combination of patterns.

Practice Session – You can try drawing fill patterns by using a pencil to draw stipple lines inside an irregular shape (see page 35). Consider children learning to write cursive; they fill entire pages with just one letter. Remember, your brain does not know the difference between drawing with a pencil or stitching at the machine – you are still developing cell memory. Fill an entire area with one shape without lifting your pencil, crossing over. or backtracking to fill the shape. The trick is to practice repeatedly. One of my instructors once said, "When you start you are not perfect, but with practice you will be perfect."

You may want to doodle larger border and sashing shapes and practice drawing borders, sashings, and block designs from pattern books, packets, and stencils. The more you practice, the better you will get. Don't get hung up on the shape. What you are aiming for is the feel of making the shape – the arm and hand motion you will be performing.

Stippling. Stippling is a commonly used fill pattern. A true stipple design's quilting is less than ¼" apart. Stipple lines are constantly curved and consistently round, and the stitching lines never touch or cross. The secret to beautiful stippling is to keep the space between the stitching lines consistent. In addition, the eye should not detect a shape. You will have your own style of stippling, like your own signature. When you stipple, begin at a place where you can cover the entire area without being boxed in, having to break your thread.

When I first practiced stippling, I found that my thread path was too random and chaotic to manage a pattern with any consistency. I had large gaps and recognizable worm shapes. So I had to develop a way to evenly fill the space and not cross over or touch another line. I did it by talking myself through it. I stitched two horizontal lines, then two vertical lines.

When I felt confident enough I would vary their length and change their angles. It took me saying, "over, back, over, back, up, down, up, down" repeatedly to finally get the kind of design I wanted.

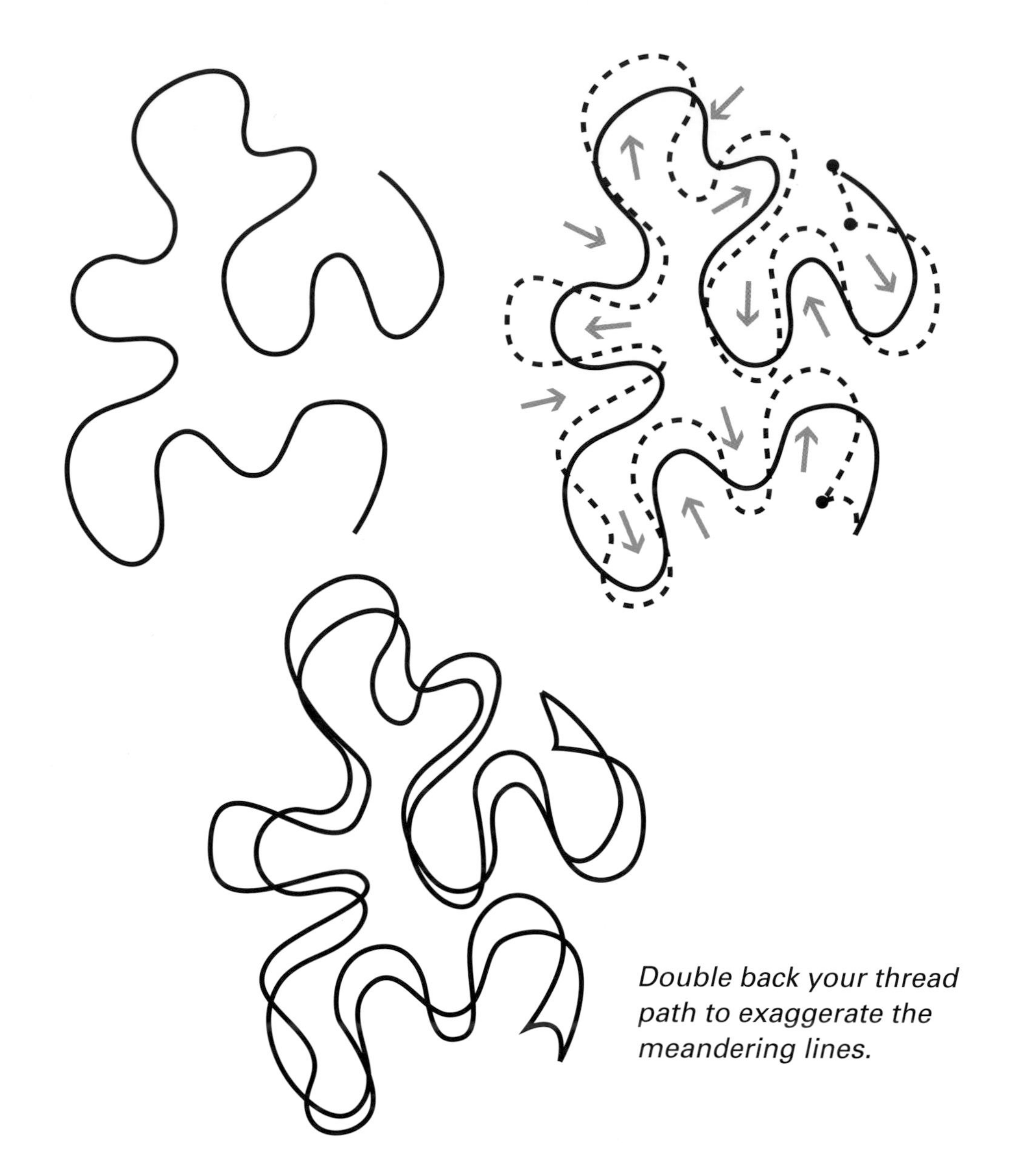

Double back your thread path to exaggerate the meandering lines.

Often we just want to get the quilting over with and take the easy way out...and meander!

Meandering. Meandering is a fill-type pattern stitched with greater than ¼" between the lines. The same ideas that apply to stippling (page 43) work for a meander pattern. Meandering is usually more open than fill work. It can consist of a single motif, such a heart, leaf, or scroll, which is repeated in different sizes and angles. Try placing an arc, loop, or S-curve between the motifs.

You can meander designs with limitless combinations of motifs. Practice them first by doodling on paper. By planning and focusing ahead, you can save your design from becoming boxed in a corner where you would have to break your thread and restart or double back. If you need to get yourself out of an area, just outline back or travel in the ditch to another area.

To virtually make your starts and stops undetectable, start and stop, enter and exit in the same place each time.

Meandering is popular because it is easy and quick and is less expensive than custom quilting. The eye should not detect a discernible repetition of lines or shapes in a meandered repetitive-shape fill pattern.

Meandering with style is when the spaced stitching is consistently shaped as well as a beautiful design. Here is an idea that will make your quilts sing, giving your quilts a design that the eye can focus on without blurring piecing lines or fabric colors. When you begin meandering, keep enough distance between thread paths so that you can double back with another meandered thread path. When you get to the end, make an arc. Then without breaking your thread, stitch the original meander in reverse; but every time the curve swings out, stitch beyond the curve, exaggerating the shape. If there is a long curve, double back and forth over it until it is time to swing out to exaggerate the next curve.

If the curve swings out to the right, the second exaggerated curve should swing to the right *beyond* it. You will quickly develop this into your own signature meander.

Freehand ideas for fills, stippling, and meandering

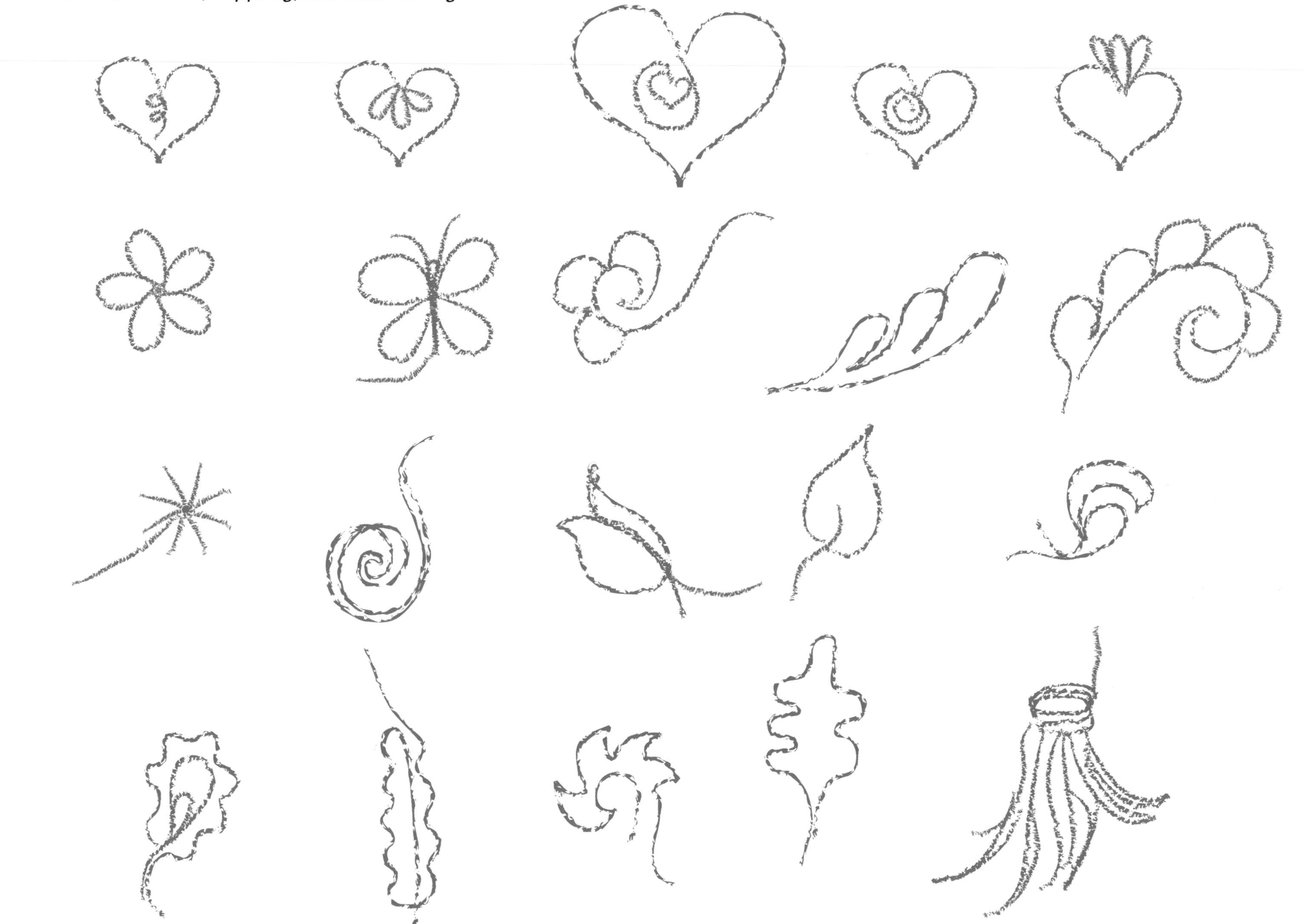

Freehand ideas for fills, stippling, and meandering

Choose three basic shapes and combine them in varying sizes to create your own custom freehand meandering pathways.

Developing Your Own Style

Your signature freehand style is easy to develop. Do you prefer making curves or straight lines? Do you end or begin your thread pathway with a curl, hook, or arc?

Here is a quick way to see how much creative style you already have with your freehand meander. Hopefully you have been doodling your way along with the practice exercises and you are comfortable drawing the five basic shapes. I think you will be surprised how much cell memory you have developed.

Practice Session – For your own freehand meander, pick two or three of the five basic shapes in the *Language of Quilting*. I chose an arc, S-curve, and straight line to practice. Start drawing them in sequence, repeating each shape three times. This is a great exercise to do in a class because each student's work is so different in style. If you like straight lines, pick a straight line and one other shape.

I use this exercise for all machine types. The secret is to make each shape pretty.

Practice Session – Have someone call out each shape in random order and draw them three times each. This is fun to do and will help you to "think with the needle," a term coined by Laura Lee Fritz.

Thinking with the Needle. Just as speakers, instructors, or comedians learn to "think on their feet," you will learn to "think with your needle." Your machine is continuously stitching, so you need to move your hands and eyes to make your stitches consistent in length, and the pattern shape continuous and lovely. The goal here is to keep stitching and not "unstitch."

Detail from NEPTUNE'S GARDEN *by Jan Hall, Eureka Pattern by Debbie Bowles, Maple Island Quilts. Quilted by Sally Terry.*

Signature Style. You can look at a quilt and instantly recognize the quilter by their signature style. For instance, my half-a-heart sashing pattern on page 14 reflects my signature style. Moreover, I started out as a quilter, not a piecer, so I have a great respect for the piecer. For that reason, I do not believe in signing my name with thread on a quilt just because I quilted it. Yet, I felt I could have a small and unobtrusive stylized signature to tuck into the design. Therefore I designed this little hand to reflect the name of my quilting business, The Quilter's Hand, and incorporate it into the quilting.

My customers make a game out of finding my little stylized hand. I would love to be a mouse in the corner when someday down the road a bunch of quilts are discovered with this mysterious little hand on them.

Signature Freehand Meander. To make your own freehand meander, pick three designs out of the choices shown on pages 45–46. Look for the five basic shapes in each design. Begin drawing them in sequence, filling the space evenly to make your own custom designed, signature freehand meander pattern. As you experiment with the different combinations, some will be easy to draw and others harder to draw. The ones you choose will be a direct reflection of you and your signature style.

The quickest way to develop your own style is to practice one shape at a time.

The GAP

Gradually Audition Patterns. How do you mull over the different quilting patterns and choose which ones to mark onto the quilt top? There is a special time during the life of a quilt when the quilt speaks to us. And it is during this part of the quilt-finishing process that many of us feel the most challenged. We agonize over process instead of embracing and trusting our creative instincts. Many of us think, "If only we had some simple step-by-step guidelines!"

The GAP. The time between completing the quilt top and starting the quilting is when you need to interpret the quilt top, choose designs, and audition patterns. The GAP is our focus. It doesn't stand for Grab a Pattern, instead it means *Gradually Audition Patterns* to meet certain goals of beauty and function.

I always enjoy this process – the time I spend with the pieced top deciding on pattern and placement. I often spend an hour drinking tea and immersing myself in the color and the patterns, admiring the maker's creativity. Join me during my favorite time, and I will share my process of making creative choices. I hope you enjoy the GAP as much as I do.

Creative Choices. If you put your quilt under the needle and just start quilting, you are what I call a non-planner. If you start the process by analyzing the style, sketching quilting motifs and spending time with the quilt top, you are a planner. Just so you are aware, in most cases when it comes to quilting designs, I am a non-planner. My dearest quilting friend is a planner. To get the results I want, though, I learned that I must plan as well. This book is for both the planner and the non-planner. Now that you have developed your own style, you can easily go from pattern to freehand, using the five shapes of the *Language of Quilting* to determine creative choices.

A B C-1 2 3

The A B C-1 2 3 Method of Selecting Designs. I call this method A B C-1 2 3 instead of "A B C, large, medium, small," because A B C rhymes with 1-2-3, and besides, it is too cumbersome to say it the other way. The key to A B C-1 2 3 is to make sure that the patterns are compatible by choosing patterns that contain at least two or three shapes in common. By using just three patterns in three different sizes, you eliminate a lot of confusion and deliberation.

Choose three different yet compatible quilting patterns and designate the patterns as A, B, and C. [Editorial note: For review, refer to size and counting consistency (page 15) and patterns that have a similar feel (page 39).]

•Choose the pattern for **large areas**. *This will be number 1.*
•Choose the pattern for **medium-sized areas**. *This will be number 2.*
•Choose the pattern for **small areas**. *This will be number 3.*

Let us say that –

- Pattern A will work best in the **blocks and borders**, which are the largest area. Therefore, that becomes A1 (Pattern A, size 1 large);
- Pattern B works in **sashings and setting triangles**, and other medium-sized areas. That becomes B2 (Pattern B, size 2 or medium);
- Pattern C, will be the **background and fill patterns**, which are usually the smallest of the three sizes. That is now C3 (Pattern C, size 3 or small). Fills are the easiest to decide on because most patterns will have a recognizable fill shape in their design.

You can also use the patterns in other sizes. For example, if you wanted to use Pattern A as a sashing strip, just reduce it and call it A2. The important thing to remember is to choose only three patterns, and to make sure that they have at least two or three of the five basic shapes in common. Then when you use them on the quilt, they will coordinate with each other, making the quilt one cohesive piece.

A circle is the best use of a shape to fill a square.

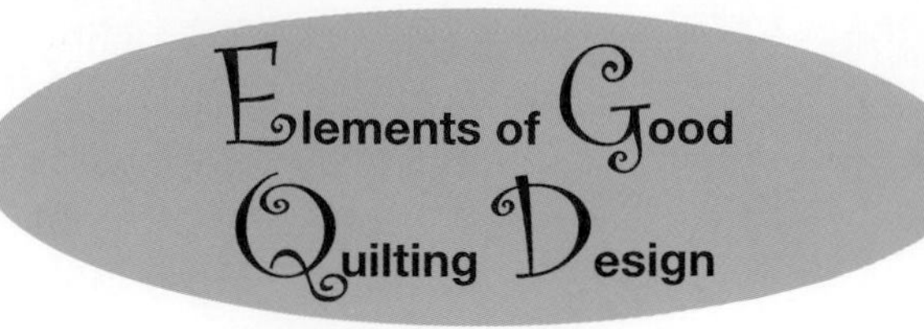

When you make design choices, you will know if you like or dislike the design; yet, you cannot quite put it into words. Most quilting instructors have a good background in design, yet do not have time to teach much design in class. Instead, they coach and guide you to make good design choices. Now with this simple review of good design elements, when you make a design choice, you will have a much better idea why you made it.

Consider this chapter as valuable as a good book on color. You no doubt have several on your bookshelf. This information is just as important to quilting patterns as color theory is to piecing.

There are five design elements basic to all art forms: contrast, balance, simplicity, scale, and repetition. To make them easy to remember, I gave them the acronym CBSSR, pronounced See-Bee-Esser. If you refer to them as CBSSR, it will help you remember to consider and apply their principles to your quilt tops, as well as to quilting patterns.

Contrast. Straight lines emphasize curves and curves emphasize straight lines. We see this with patterns such as straight-line crosshatching behind curved appliqué shapes. Providing contrast with pattern, size, line, texture, and color can add movement and excitement to the quilt.

Balance. An even distribution of quilting lines, thread colors and pattern shapes, balance is using straight lines to emphasize curves and curves to emphasize straight lines. A small area of heavy quilting equals a large area of light quilting.

Simplicity. Plain lines without embellishment are tastefully elegant, quick to execute, and easy to quilt. The best example of overall simplicity is the stunning Amish quilt.

Scale. This refers to the size of the quilting design in relation to the quilt's measurement, the block, and the fabric pattern. This is the easiest of all design elements to see and adjust. We can get clues as to how close or far apart to space thread paths from the size of the individual pieces in each block.

Repetition. When patterns are used repeatedly and in different sizes, recurring patterns form texture and are useful for filling the background. This technique is very effective on large-scale borders. Areas of a quilt with dense print and color patterns can be so strong that stitched quilting designs are not discernible. When this occurs, pattern repetition works well, making texture.

In the designs shown at the right, the quilting pattern is about the same size and has similar angles to the pieced block. Also, when angles, curves, and other design elements are too similar to the block piecing, the patterns will blend and ultimately be lost.

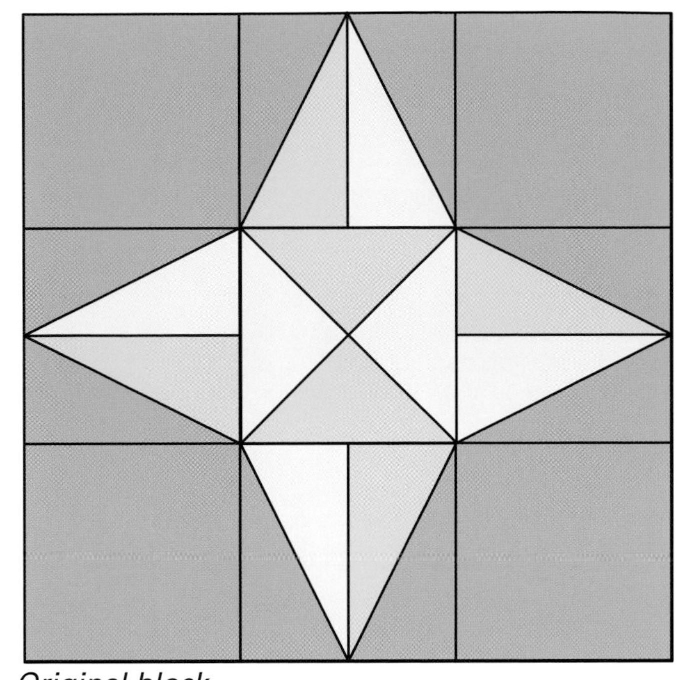

Original block

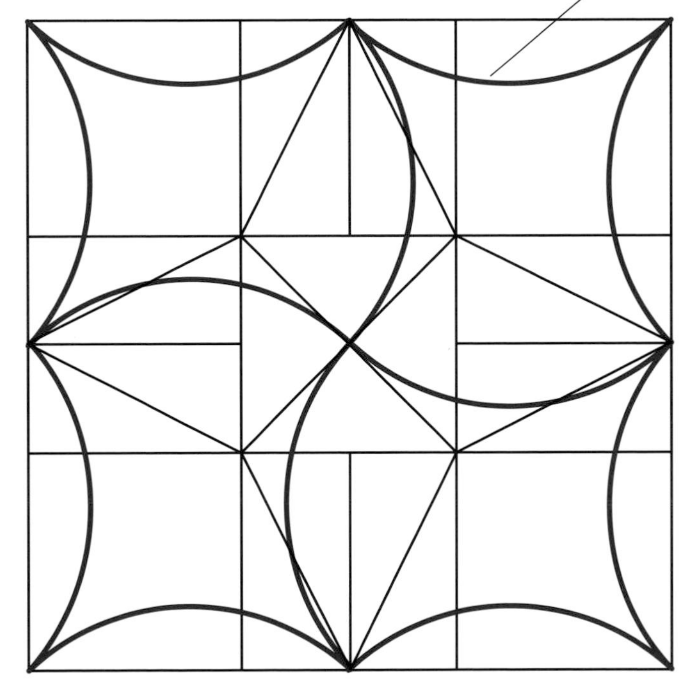

Good design scale, contrast and balance

Bad design, scale and contrast

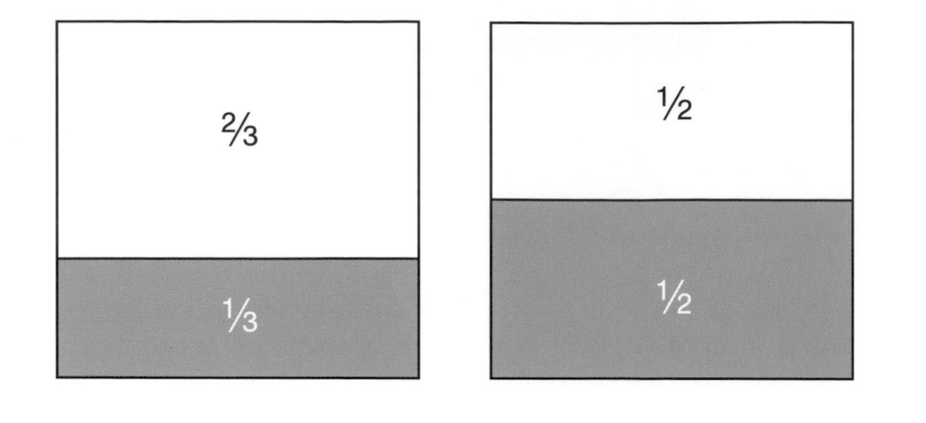

Be mindful of negative space around the edge of the design. When a motif is too large for the area, the design may go all the way out to the edges of the block. The quilting design goes into the piecing line and the piecing pattern gets lost.

Odd numbers are more pleasing to the eye than even numbers. This is especially true in nature; just think how many leaves a rose bush has – five or three or one. Using odd numbers also makes the quilting design easier to execute because it lacks symmetry (mirrored images).

Design Decisions

Have you ever considered this? The same kinds of choices that we need to make for piecing are also appropriate for the quilting patterns; they are directly related.

- Balancing the fabrics in a typical quilt top relates directly to balancing the quilting pattern.
- The feature fabric is equivalent to the feature block and border patterns.
- The plain fabric is used for the fill pattern that create soft shadowed textures.
- A small print fabric equates to the sashing and setting triangles.
- Using geometric-patterned fabric is similar to the use of repeated shapes created by straight or curved lines as in crosshatching, railroad, hanging diamonds, Baptist Fan, and other simple, repeated geometric shapes.

The Golden Mean. For centuries, artists have used the Golden Mean to create a "pleasing to the eye" division of space. The Golden Mean divides space into thirds. We see this daily in professional photography and find it even in the way we dress. Look in fashion magazines and you will see ⅓ top with ⅔ skirt or pants showing, ⅔ jacket with ⅓ skirt showing. Imagine ½ top with ½ skirt showing. That would have an unattractive and boring effect, especially on me!

Use The Golden Mean to visually balance colors, light and dark values, and shapes. Use it also to divide a large border into thirds instead of halves. A border divided in half is difficult to achieve accurately, and it's obvious when you have been less than successful; imperfections are less obvious if the space is divided into thirds. It is easier to focus your eye on a border that is divided into thirds than one that is divided in half. To learn how to measure perfect intervals in a space, please see **Appendix A** on page 89.

Scrappy quilts scream for ordered texture. Use a design with ordered texture, like the Baptist Fan, on scrappy quilt tops, on quilts with unrelated blocks, and on heavily printed colorful fabrics. The fact that a lot of quilting does not show up on large-scale, dense prints was a hard lesson for me to learn. I spent hours creating beautiful patterns to quilt on colorful printed fabrics, but the patterns are only visible in the half hour of twilight between certain latitudes three days a year! Scrappy quilts require an organized pattern of repetition to create balance. The eye needs something to focus on and the repeated rhythm of light and dark shadows that the quilting provides giving order to disarray.

The repetition that the Baptist Fan pattern creates looks beautiful on both front and back of single-block scrappy tops. I highly recommend this pattern; even when it is done freehand it is stunning. This quilt is so beautiful on the back that I always think I have two quilts, one side for summer and the other side for fall.

Sampler quilts can be a challenge for quilters. I have always enjoyed coming up with unique quilting designs for each block of a sampler quilt. I can spend hours just thinking about the possibilities. One year our quilt guild had a sampler quilt block-of-the-month challenge. The tops came in all at once for me to quilt and when they were finished, they would be entered in our yearly guild quilt show. I wanted to find a unique way to stitch each one differently.

I discovered early on that if there was a common shape in each block and I treated that shape the same way each time, the quilting went faster. For example, if each block had a square center, I would crosshatch each one. Then I outlined all triangle shapes the same way in each block. The quilt looked a lot more unified and I did not have to come up with a different idea for each block. Each quilt looks distinctive, yet the design decision is the same.

Illustrations on this page are from Electric Quilt 4.

A Baptist Fan quilting pattern looks beautiful on the front and back of scrappy quilts.

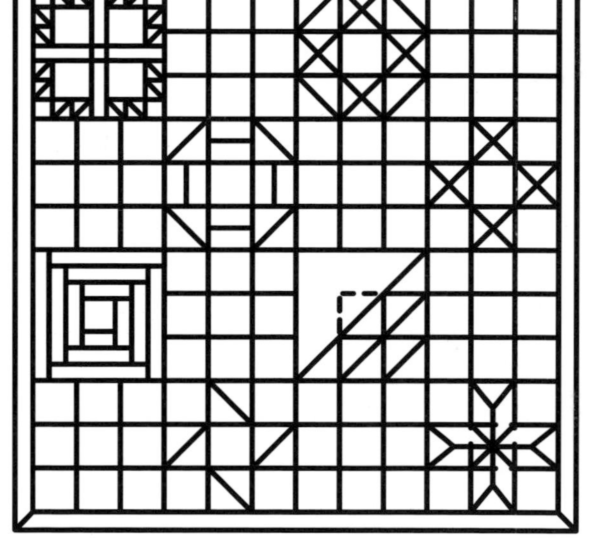

Common shapes are quilted in each block to achieve a more unified, yet distinctive, look to the sampler quilt.

Repetition is perfect for scrappy quilts and samplers.

Quilting Questions

To help with the quilting design process, I have created a series of questions. Answer them in order, and it will help you visualize the finished quilt. The answers make your decisions easier and quicker, and your creativity and confidence will increase and reduce what I call pre-quilting fretfulness.

The Five W's

Who is the recipient? Is it for charity, competition, birthday gift, college graduate, anniversary couple, the piecer's personal use, etc.?

What is the intended use? Will it be a wallhanging, bed cover, throw, baby quilt, etc.? Is it for a contest or guild challenge?

When does the quilt need to be finished? When we become rushed, we typically spend less time planning in the GAP. What if the baby comes early, the family reunion dates move up, or Aunt Martha and Uncle Robb arrive two months earlier than originally planned for an important celebration? Take heart – this step-by-step guide can help you get the quilting done in time without sacrificing quilting design.

Where will the quilt be kept? Is it destined for use in a hot, humid climate? Will it be on the sofa, hung on the wall for display, or stored in a glass trunk? Will it be with the baby at all times?

Why were the particular fabrics and block patterns chosen? Is the top constructed with old scraps? Is it a kit or block of the month? Is it romantic, country French, patriotic, historic, or artistic? Remember, rarely is the quilt top pattern chosen with specific quilting motifs in mind. Record the answers to the five W's on paper, and don't forget to find out if the recipient loves heart or feather quilting designs and dislikes leaves.

These questions need to be answered by the piecer. The answers will help you to determine the best choice of batting, backing, thread, and thread coverage. You may want to explore other sources for more technical information about products you plan to use. This information also gives you clues for quilting patterns.

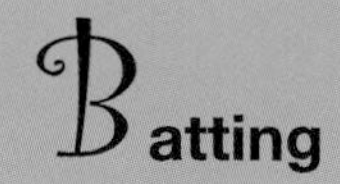

Batting

It all comes down to personal taste in choosing batting. Always read the information about the batting before you decide which is best suited for the quilt. Look for content, loft, shrinkage, maximum distance between stitches, suitability for hand and/or machine quilting, and suitability under light or dark fabrics.

To prevent the batting from poking through the backing of the quilt, make sure the scrim, heat-sealed bonded or resin side, is down and against the backing. The various methods of sealing the batting prevents it from migrating through to the back when the needle takes a stitch. It takes close examination to find the sealed side. Also, if it is needle-punched, making it easier to sew through, look at the needle punch holes and make sure that the sewing needle is going into the batting in the same direction as the needle punches.

When I use two layers of batting for extra loft, I place the top batting sealed side up and the bottom batting sealed side down.

Batt Questions & Answers

- **Does the batt need pre-washing?**
  I recommend hand washing the batt.
- **Is a soft batting important?**
  Certain garments and quilts require a supple drape.
- **Do you want a puffy look?**
  Comforter-style quilts, or quilts with a great deal of beautiful pattern work may need lofty batting.
- **Do you want a flat look?**
  A flat antique look is wonderful in bed quilts, heritage-style quilts, and for quilt restoration. If you are quilting a wallhanging, keep in mind that it is not normally washed and needs to contain a batting which hangs flat and will not sag over time, yet needs to have a loft to see the 3-D design. Batting also has a grain, so use the lengthwise – less stretch – grain in wallhangings for strength.
- **Will it take a lot of wear?**
  Dorm quilts, baby quilts, and utility quilts all take a lot of wear and require a lot of cleaning. They need batting that will stand up to washing, detergent, and drying. For baby quilts I recommend all-cotton fabric, thread, and batting for fire safety.
- **Does it need to be warm?**
  Consider weight and fiber content for different degrees of warmth. Wool and silk actually breathe and are as light-weight and warm as a very dense polyester that does not breathe.

Ask for more information from individual batting manufacturers regarding polyester, scrimmed and unscrimmed cotton, bonded and unbonded wool, or silk.

Backing

The color choice of the backing will affect the finished look. Most professional machine quilters match the bobbin thread color to the top thread work. When the thread does not match the backing fabric and batting is thin, threads can show through to the other side. Keep in mind what it would it look like with white bobbin thread on a dark top!

The *Creative Thread Guide* (Resources, page 93), my thread video, talks about choosing bobbin thread colors when using variegated threads.

Backing Questions & Answers

To wash or not to wash the backing?

I usually wash the backing if the top fabric is washed. This allows the contents to shrink the same, although the verdict is still out.

Will the quilt be receiving a lot of use?

A darker-colored backing may be preferable because it will show less dirt and stains.

Is it meant to be a wallhanging?

For quilts that will hang, consider constructing the backing with the fabric grain (which runs parallel to the selvage edge) running from top to bottom. This allows for more strength and less stretch over time. If the quilt is a wallhanging, the backing may not be noticeable at all.

Is the thread work most important?

A solid-colored backing will highlight good thread work, while a printed backing will disguise the thread work and make it less noticeable.

Do you want to use a special fabric?

If you have a prized piece of fabric that you do not wish to cut up, use it for the backing. Remember that high quality printed fabrics also come in wide widths for backing. There is now new batik fabric that is 108" wide, perfect for backing. See Resources, page 93.

Should I save money using an inexpensive fabric?

No, low quality backing fabric has no resiliency. Consider the amount spent on the quilt top fabric. Shouldn't the backing get the same consideration? Use extra blocks, trial blocks, and scrap fabric (a great stash depleter) to piece the backing. Then you can buy more fabric!

Are bed sheets all right to use for backing?

No, they are a poor choice for backing for a number of reasons. They usually contain some polyester, which does not shrink the same as cotton; the thread count is usually much greater than the quilt top; and the bobbin thread lays on top of the sheet instead of becoming part of it because of thread count density.

Is additional backing fabric needed?

The outer dimension of the backing as it rolls on the take-up roller is greater than the inner dimension of the quilt top and needs additional backing fabric as it is quilted. For example, pick up a magazine and consider the cover as the quilt top; the pages, the batting, and the back of the magazine are the quilt backing material. Roll the magazine into a tube with the cover on the inside and the back of the magazine on the outside. Notice how much shorter the back of the magazine is than the cover. That is why we need additional backing fabric.

For overall size, are there other considerations?

Method of quilting

Allow for extra backing and additional shrinkage when the batting is high loft and the quilt will be loaded on a longarm or shortarm system. Add 6–8" to each dimension if loading on a frame. The more quilting, the more the quilt dimensions are reduced.

Piecing

Purchase enough backing fabric so that when pieced together, it is at least four inches greater in both width and length than the quilt top measurement.

Shrinkage

Buy enough to allow for the backing fabric to shrink if washed and dried.

Binding

Have you thought how the binding color affects the quilt? I feel we tend to overlook binding considerations. I suggest that you experiment with different binding colors, along with pattern styles, before deciding. Often times we settle on the obvious when there are other choices that could be more exciting.

- Use a binding color that **blends** with the border to allow the eye to rest and linger in the border area, especially those borders made with incredible appliqué work or complicated piecing.
- A **contrast** binding not only stops a busy fabric or piecing design, it also visually contains the quilt. A contrast color, when used for the binding, will make the eye bounce back to the main body of the quilt.
- Use a **black** binding to contain the busy movement when the quilt has a busy, scrappy, overall block pattern.
- Use a **single** binding on fashion garments to reduce bulk.
- Use a **wider** binding on heavier quilts made with flannel or fleece fabric.
- Art quilts may require a very **narrow** binding, or an envelope finish, so the binding does not compete with the design elements.
- Take care that the binding fabric **complements** the top in color, texture, and cleaning.
- Allow an overhang of two inches all the way around the quilt when the back is brought around to the front of the quilt top for a **self-binding**.

Whimsey by Jan Hall from Whimsical Triangles Pattern by JoAnn Belling. Quilted by Sally Terry.

Experiment with different binding colors before you choose.

The Overall Effect

Questions to be answered by the fabric. There are five more questions that you need to answer about the quilt before you can start planning the quilting design. Refer to the previous information on batting (page 57), backing (page 59), and binding (page 61) when answering the questions.

Are both the piecing and fabric traditional?

This type of quilt may take the least amount of quilting using traditional quilting patterns. The stitching paths usually stay consistently two inches to three inches apart. You will be able to take clues from the size of the piecing shapes. The more traditional quilting patterns of large feather wreaths and parallel lines are common. Consider that cotton thread or dull polyester thread is often used. Cotton thread is a good choice along with thin cotton batting for a traditional look.

Is the piecing traditional and the fabric contemporary?

The more contemporary the quilt look becomes, the more quilting it needs. Different areas may need to be treated differently within the same quilt. Contemporary fabrics can have bright neon colors with graphic or geometric designs. Regardless of design, they often have solid bold color areas. Bright rayon, shiny polyester and variegated threads work well, while quilting patterns are tighter, more varied.

Are both the piecing and fabric contemporary?

You will need to add even more surface coverage and embellishment to contemporary quilts. The quilting will reflect the piecing shapes and fabric designs. Often contemporary quilts scream for decorative threads and lots of it. Many times the piecing is totally ignored and tight custom meandering is featured. Quilting lines tend to become more angular in contemporary quilts.

Is this a story or art quilt?

It will need custom quilting all the way if it's a unique art quilt. When the quilt is pictorial the quilting patterns enhance the theme. There is no limit to the imagination when it comes to thread. Free-hand embroidery is used to emphasize areas.

Do you want a special design?

Is it for trapunto or wholecloth, is it an heirloom top, half completed? When this is the case, quilting will take time and may require extra steps to complete the project. I tend to reflect the overall look in a very conservative way and try to feature the quilt top and piecing rather than the thread.

Use the thousands of resources that can inspire and help you make decisions. Visit your local fabric shop, the library, and don't forget the Internet. We are still in the GAP, though, and we still have a blank canvas to fill.

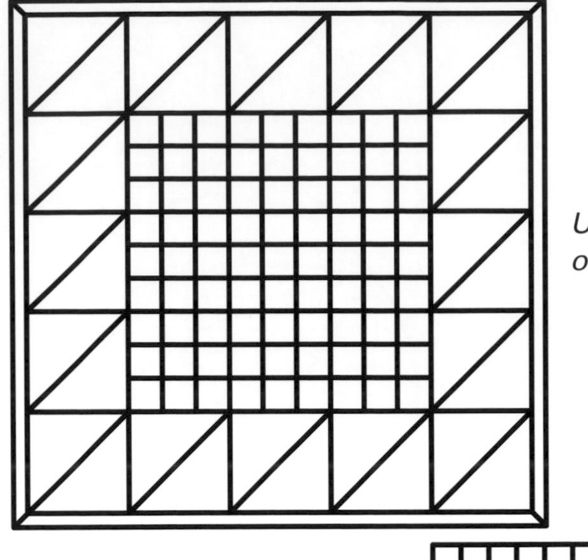

Underquilted border, overquilted body

Overquilted border, underquilted body

To prevent wavy borders, make sure that the thread density is consistent over the whole quilt. If the border is more densely quilted than the body of the quilt, the body of the quilt will billow out. When the body is overquilted and borders underquilted, borders become wavy because of the unquilted fabric.

The following is another list of questions that you must ask yourself as you prepare to quilt. These decisions will be determined by the quilt top. Keep this list nearby when you are in the GAP; they are a reference pathway to use again and again. Remember that the rules of CBSSR apply here.

Quilting Density. Observing the piecing and fabric designs will help determine how much quilting needs to be done. We already know that non-traditional quilts require more quilting than traditional ones, and densely-printed fabrics won't show the quilting as much as plain ones.

Consider the batting loft that you will use. Check the batting manufacturer's recommendation for thread spacing. Remember to ask the customer's preference here, too. (Refer to batting suggestions on page 57.)

Next, look at the size of the pieces. For instance, because the pieces in a Log Cabin quilt are usually quite narrow, if you choose to stitch-in-the-ditch, the thread paths will be relatively close together.

Consider the type of thread to be used. Decorative and variegated threads contrast with the strong fabric colors and influence a more creative approach.

I will normally quilt the border of the quilt last. The density of the quilting in the body will determine the density in the borders. My ideas usually change halfway through the quilting and give a clearer picture of what is needed in the border.

Illustrations on this page are from Electric Quilt 4.

Stitching-in-the-Ditch. Use a lighter-weight thread and stitch-in-the-ditch on the low side of the pressed seam. Stitched-in-the-ditch shapes appear to come forward; surrounding areas recede when filled with background quilting. This technique gives dimension to wallhangings, it accents a center medallion, and sets off border appliqué.

Patchwork. To ensure the finished quilt is squared up and the sides are equal, stitch-in-the-ditch on both sides of the sashing. I learned that the sashing is the skeleton of the quilt. If you are machine quilting with a traditional machine, Mabeth Oxenrider teaches to stitch-in-the-ditch all the way around the sashing first, then quilt the body of the quilt the way you normally would. This will assure a squared up quilt because the basting of the quilt sandwich holds it square initially, and the stitching-in-the-ditch keeps it that way. On the longarm I like to ditch the sashing and the main areas as I go. It will reinforce the quilt whether it hangs on the wall or accompanies an active two-year-old.

Specialty Work or Trapunto. Trapunto patterns will set the quilting tone and theme and require special handling. Art quilts will have more abstract quilting designs. Appliqué blocks are more pictorial and need contrast; memory quilts and picture quilts invite personal words, symbols, or other memorable objects.

Solid Areas or Plain Fabric. Locate areas with a minimum of pattern. These are the best areas to feature quilting designs. Look for them and plan the rest of the quilting around these plain fabric areas. Use thread with a heavier weight here to make the quilting patterns more visible.

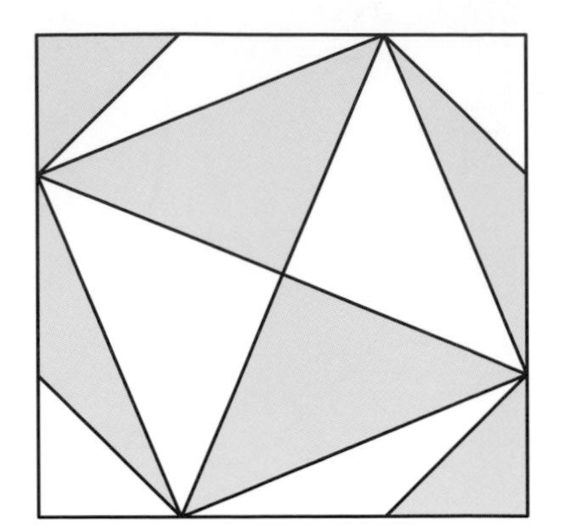

Look for the secondary pattern formed when blocks are joined and then quilt to fill that shape. This is an excellent example of strong secondary shapes.

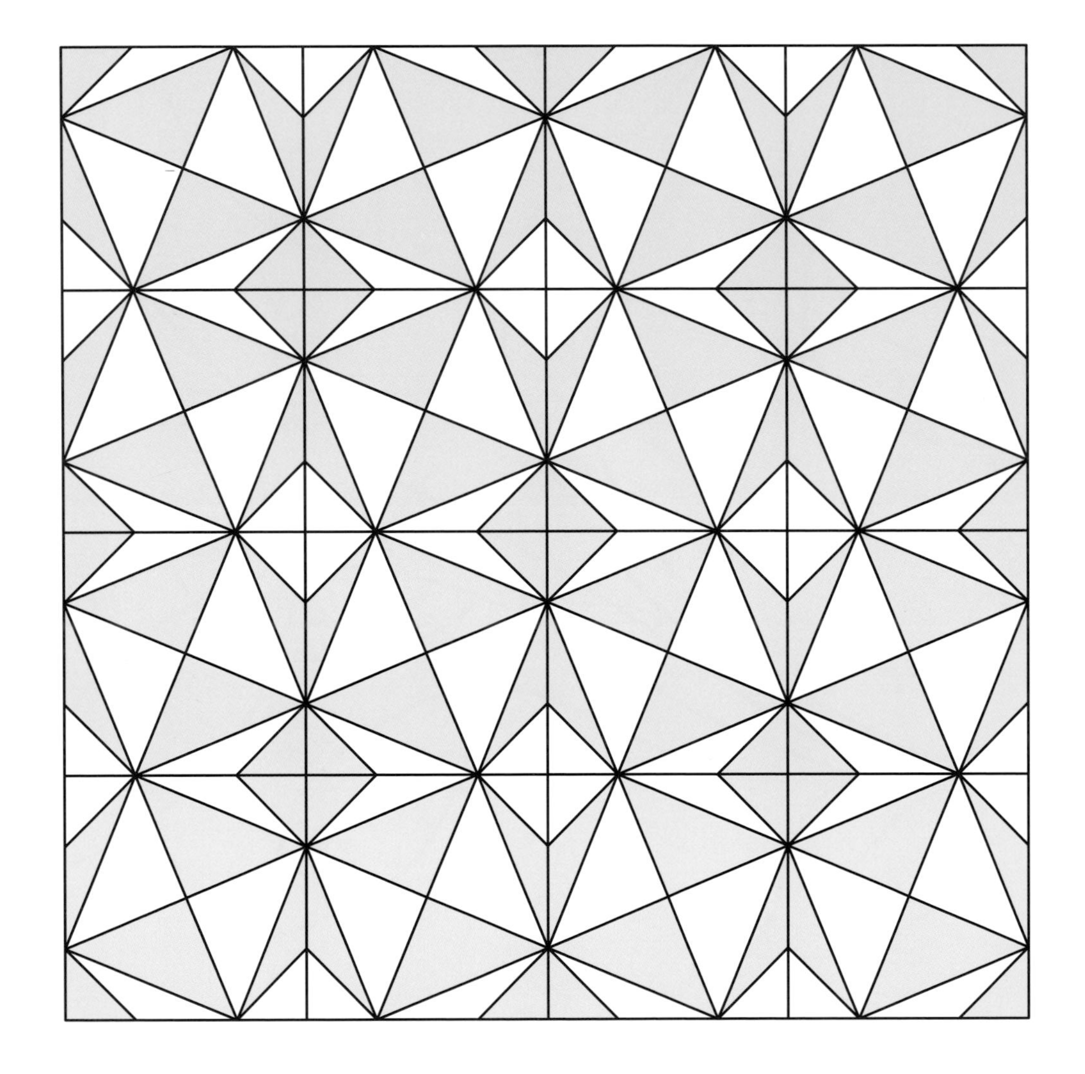

Secondary Pattern. When the block patterns form another secondary pattern, choose a quilting pattern to fit that shape. If secondary patterns are hard to see, squint, look at the quilt through the wrong end of binoculars, or take a photograph of the quilt top in either black-and-white or color.

Element of Layers. Look for a 3-D quality where areas float over or under the primary block pattern. These layers are often found behind appliqué, in the corners of four adjacent blocks, and are sometimes accidentally created by the uniqueness of block patterns. Use larger patterns, crosshatching, or decorative, repetitive, geometric, or linear quilting to make several smaller shapes look like one large shape.

Dividing Spaces. Take cues from the piecing and continue those lines into adjacent larger areas and even across into the border. I will often extend shapes right into the border. As always, large plain areas need more quilting to balance the block patterns, and the batting needs to be tacked down and secured. Sometimes I will make phantom blocks appear or use the miniature version of another pattern already in the quilt to break up a larger space. Keep plenty of small patterns around like the ones shown throughout the book – most are continuous-line, and are perfect for small areas. (See Resources, page 93, *Think Small* by Power Publications.)

Illustrations on this page are from Electric Quilt 4.

Sometimes the blocks and fabrics are so spectacular that the quilt does not need a lot of quilting. It may only require stitch-in-the-ditch thread work. In that case, I suggest stitching-in-the-ditch with a reflective specialty thread like Mylar holographic ribbon or a variegated metallic thread to add a subtle shimmer that helps to feature the piecing.

Borders

When borders are wide, stitching them parallel from end to end divides the area into more manageable sections for quilting. I remember one quilt where each border had a small appliqué design. I divided off the area with a perpendicular stitching line to the edge on each side of the appliqué and crosshatched behind it, continuing the border pattern until I came to the next appliquéd area. The quilting set off the appliqué and accented the border at the same time.

When the quilt does not have a border, it is easy to create one by treating the outside row of blocks as the border and quilting them with a distinctive design. This gives more interest to the quilt. You can also create phantom sashings when quilt blocks are large and the area between the pieced patterns can be organized into a secondary design.

I also like to add an additional layer of pattern to setting and corner triangles. This seems to frame the body of the quilt and keeps the eye from traveling off the edge of the quilt. If the fabric in the corner and setting triangles is a busy print, fanned lines work well.

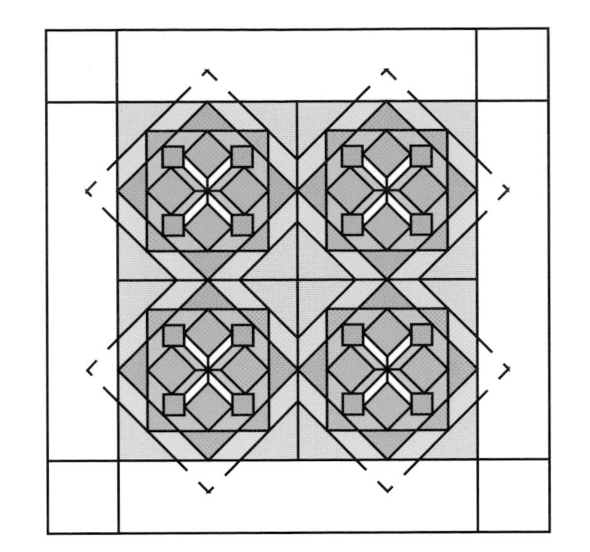

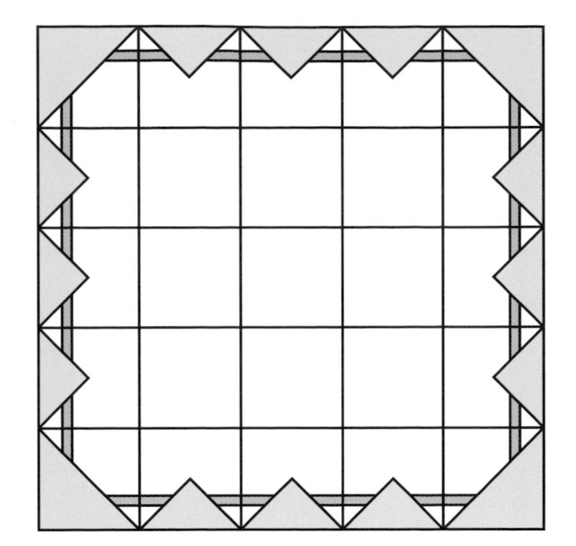

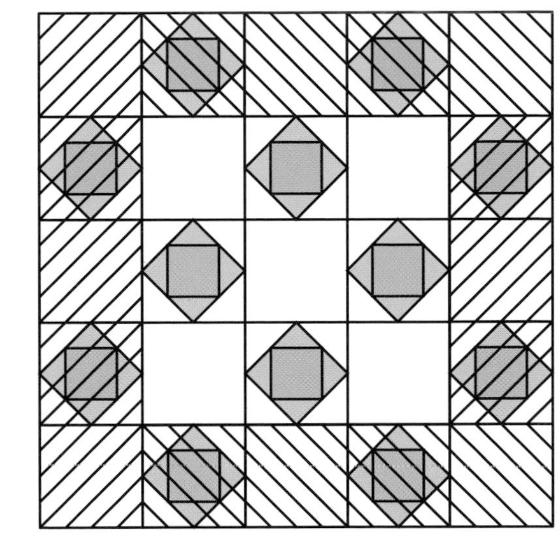

Illustrations on this page are from Electric Quilt 4.

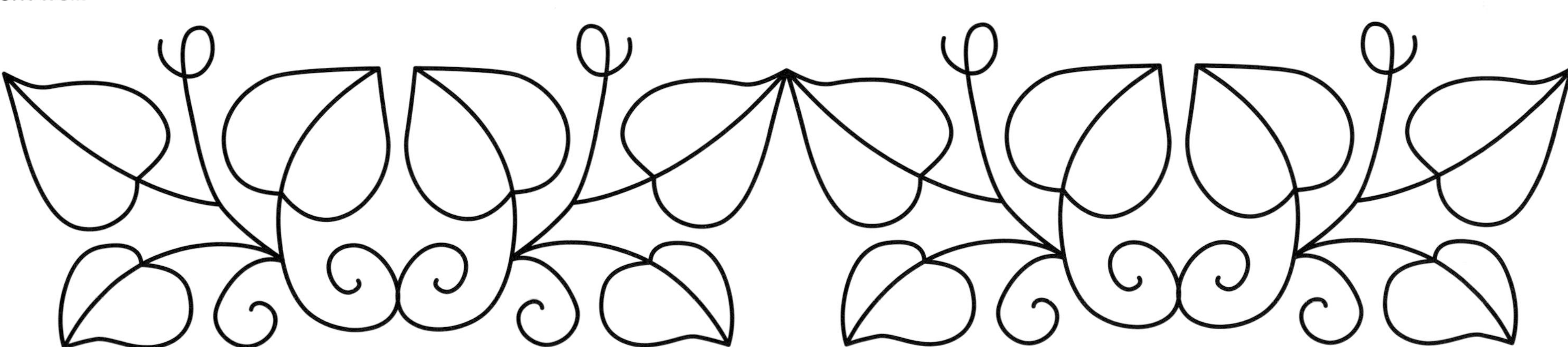

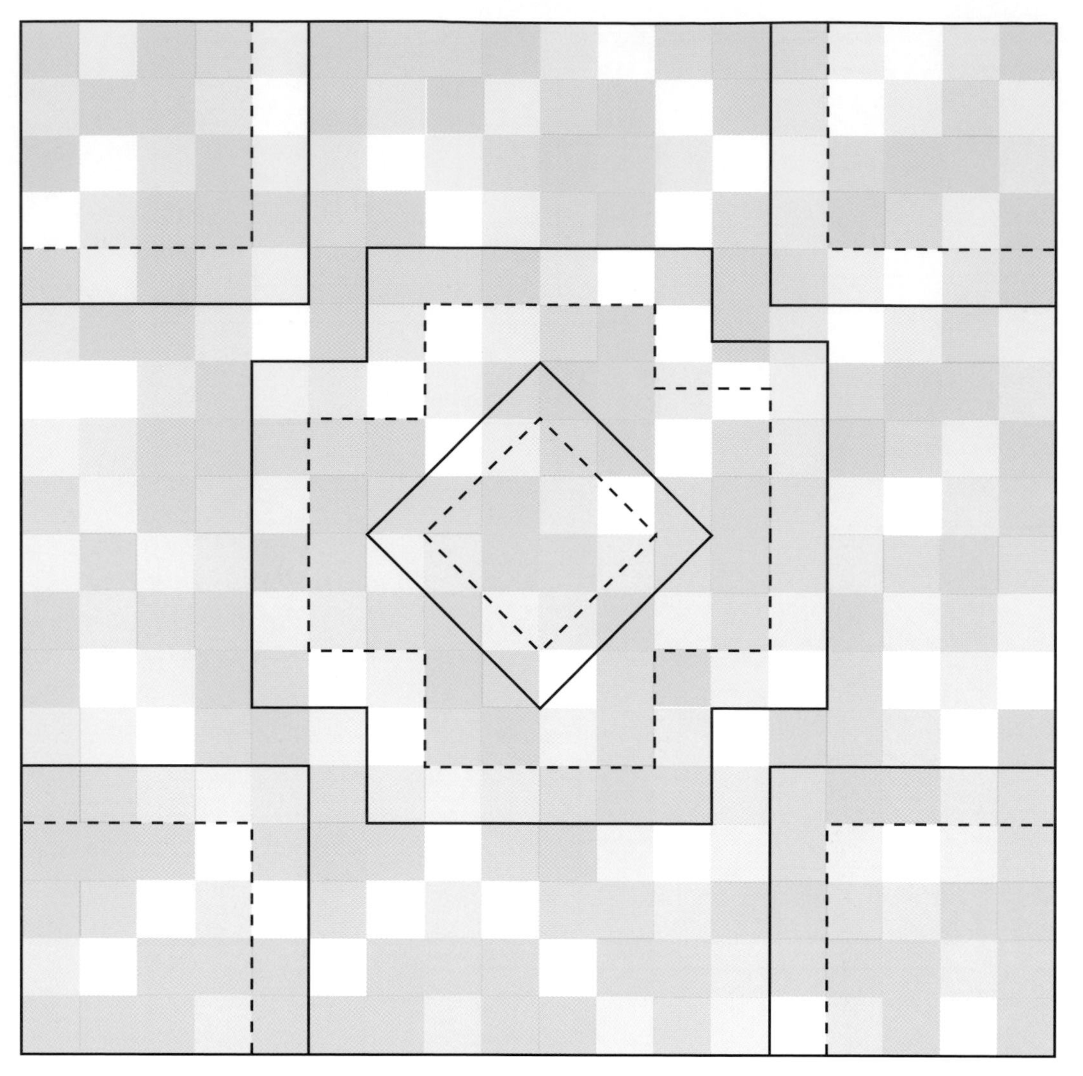

To tie together scrappy quilts with a single block pattern, or charm quilts made with just one shape, use the piecing lines. Starting from the center, create one large block pattern over the entire surface of the quilt. It is best to make double stitching lines an inch or two apart.

Remember that thread appears lighter on the quilt than on the spool. When you are starting out, match the thread color to the fabric to hide bobbles as well as starts and stops.

Thread

The previous questions should help you visualize the style of quilting motifs required. The next step is to audition your chosen quilting patterns and threads.

Get out the thread and let it inspire you. Auditioning thread is just as important as auditioning patterns, because your understanding of the quilt top is reflected in the thread as well as in the quilting pattern. Have fun trying a variety of threads; they are sure to spark an idea.

To audition thread, pull off a yard or two and place it on the quilt top. Scrunch it up to mimic the density of the quilting pattern, then squint at it. Try several different colors, including solids and variegated varieties as well as specialty threads.

Color. I often use purple threads on burgundy fabric and burgundy threads on purple fabric, orange on red, etc. It is easy to see and it excites the eye. When the contrast in color on a quilt top is dramatic, try a variegated thread containing many of the colors in the top to tie contrasting areas together. Variegated threads also tie together warm and cool colors, and multicolor threads bring an errant color swatch back into the fold.

Varieties. There are many varieties of threads available today, and most of them are used in all types of sewing machines – from longarms to shortarm systems to embroidery machines. Some threads work better when the machine runs slowly, while others work well stitching fast. Some specialty threads like Mylar holograph ribbon are not heat sensitive and are dried in a dryer and ironed. Some threads are not colorfast and are not recommended for frequently washed quilts. Your local thread dealer can give you more information, or you can refer to the numerous books about threads.

Video. Another good source of information is the *Creative Thread Guide* video; it covers 25 different top thread changes and 20 bobbin weight changes. If you are fearful of running thread, this video will give you confidence and encouragement. See Resources, page 93, for information on how to order.

Now we are ready to discuss the different styles of quilting patterns available and talk about the pros and cons of each.

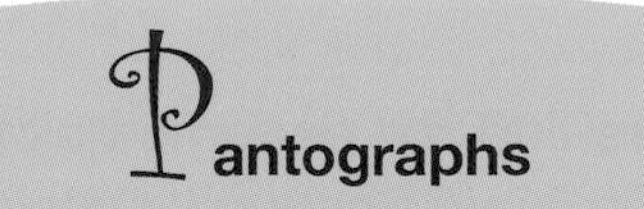

antographs

erns and Pantographs. When audi-
ese single- or multiple- continuous-line
keep in mind that rolls usually come
feet long and 3 to 18 inches wide. The
d for pantograph is "pan" as in pan-
ongarm-machine quilters, shortarm
r quilters using a home quilting system
tographs or roll patterns on a table at
of their machine; then they hand guide
or laser-light pointer over the pattern
ng the machine and stitching the pat-
the quilt.

l machine and hand quilters often use
ns because it's such a quick and easy
ark and stitch. Simply lay out the roll
nd mark the entire length of a border at
Roll pattern, including book form and
acks, are listed in Resources, page 93.

ok of it this way –
tylus is the needle
longarm, midarm,
shortarm systems.

Thread coverage and fiber content are very important considerations. Remember that the needle goes up and down one time for every two times the bobbin goes around on a rotary hook machine; once for the hook to catch the thread and once more to complete the stitch. Therefore, top thread goes up and down through the needle-eye 50 to 100 times before burying in the quilt, depending on the distance the take-up arm travels, the diameter of the thread and stitch length. The bobbin thread, on the other hand, goes directly into the fabric. That is why we *bobbin paint* with many threads we cannot run through the needle.

Traditional machines stitch from 500 times a minute and up. Industrial machines stitch 3500 stitches per minute and higher for longarm or shortarm systems. Think how strong the thread must be to pound through all those layers of fabrics and batting.

Polyester Threads. These can create friction resulting in heat. The friction also heats the needle up to 600°, causing polyester and other synthetic threads to stretch. They will shrink to their original length when cool.

Natural Fiber Threads. Natural fiber threads, such as linen, wool, cotton, and silk are not heat sensitive and adjust with the natural movement and fiber content of the quilt. I prefer to run like thread fibers on the top and in the bobbin, which match the fiber contents of the batting. In addition, I firmly believe you can run any thread combinations that result in little breakage and a quality stitch.

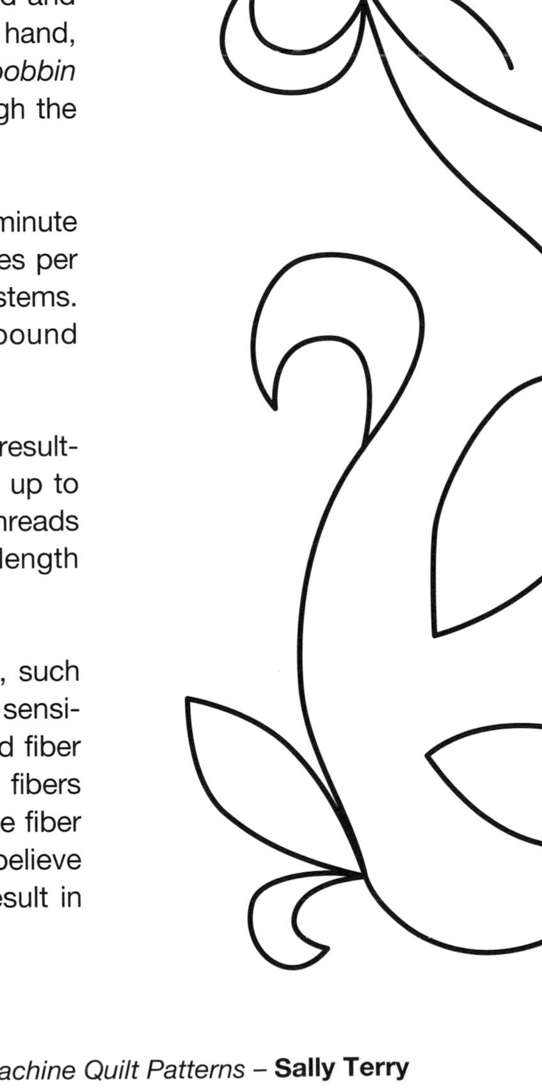

Rayon Thread. Rayon thread is cellulose-based, made from trees. At one time rayon lacked strength and was not color fast, although it was prized for its sheen and beautiful colors. Today many rayon threads come in an enormous array of hues, are color fast, and strong enough to run high-speed on a longarm without breaking.

Monofilament and Nylon Threads. These types of threads can be run either on the top or in the bobbin but are not recommended in both. They are favored for their transparency, which adapts to any fabric color and becomes nearly invisible. It is used on art quilts in the bobbin to eliminate bobbin thread changes, and as a top thread on highly colored blocks and fabrics. Any thread type can run in combination with monofilament. It comes in several shades, including clear for very light fabrics, smoke, and the newer dull finish. Monofilament thread is also available in colors. It is simply a matter of personal preference to run this type of thread.

I consider thread selection and proper tension to be so important that I have made a thread video, the *Creative Thread Guide*, for personal and professional use (see Resources, page 93). The 12 Points for Choosing Threads, page 70, are demonstrated in the video.

12 Points for Choosing Threads

- Remember to always choose a very high quality thread that is consistently smooth.
- Traditional quilts require less pattern and thread. Always check the batting information for the recommended distance between stitches.
- Utility quilts need stronger thread, smaller stitches, and greater overall stitching to stand up to the rigors of cleaning. Excessively laundered quilts need strong polyester or cotton-based threads.
- Long stitch lengths tend to be weaker. The industry average is 8–14 stitches per inch. On my longarm machine, I average about eleven stitches per inch. Stitches spaced less than eight per inch tend to break when stressed.
- If I want the stitches to be seen or decorative, like continuous-line redwork with 12-wt. cotton thread, I will use eight stitches per inch. I will also use eight stitches per inch for mylar holographic ribbon. It looks like hand stitching when threaded flat.
- Choose small diameter thread to hide stitch-in-the-ditch work along seam lines and for tighter stippling.
- The more contemporary the block and fabric, the more thread and stitching is neede The opposite is also true. A tr tional quilt pattern usually re less thread.
- Many decorative threads are coated to run easier and wor hangings and art quilts. Th are available and make thre through the sewing machine.
- Choose larger diameter thr quilting pattern. Many manuf more than one thread weight.
- Variegated threads are easy terned fabric and are very pop
- Some threads run better slo higher speeds. Just changing in less breakage and a nicer s
- Cross-wound threads should Smooth-wound threads shoul

If your thread breaks three times in a row after running well for some time, check for lint in the bobbin area.

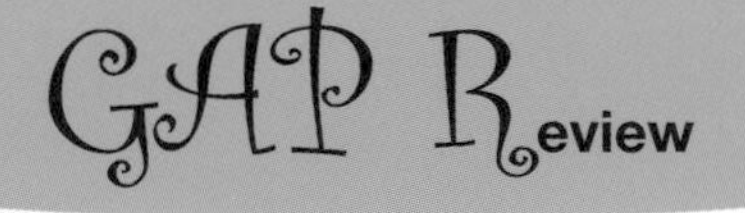

GAP Review

You now have all the pathways. The list here sum questions you need to have answered in one sm them of yourself, and your customer, each time you

Remember **The Five W's:** Who is the recipient intended use? Where will the quilt be kept? When need to be finished? Why were these fabrics and chosen?

Determine **the overall quilting effect.** By looking and piecing shapes, select the design that will those choices.

Think about **CBSSR** to influence all your design decis

- **Contrast**
- **Balance**
- **Simplicity**
- **Repetiti**

Visualize the finished quilt by answering the e that will help you make decisions quickly and easi must the quilting be, considering traditional or r piecing and fabric designs? Is specialty work or t ed? Where are the solid areas of plain fabric? Do t areas connect and form a secondary pattern? Is th of layers, areas that float over or continue unde Where is the smaller, beautifully pieced work to b the-ditch? Where are the larger spaces that you into smaller sections? Does it need a border or sas

Pathways to Quilting Specific Patterns

The more you look at quilts, the more you will begin seeing shapes you can quilt to create interest and beauty. This book is designed to help you see quilt tops in a whole new way.

In this section we will travel pathways through some of the most recognizable quilt block patterns and discuss some ideas for quilting designs. This is the process that makes me so passionate about quilting. Use these suggestions as you spend time choosing quilting designs.

I hope you will feel inspired and enjoy the creative process of being in the GAP as much as I do.

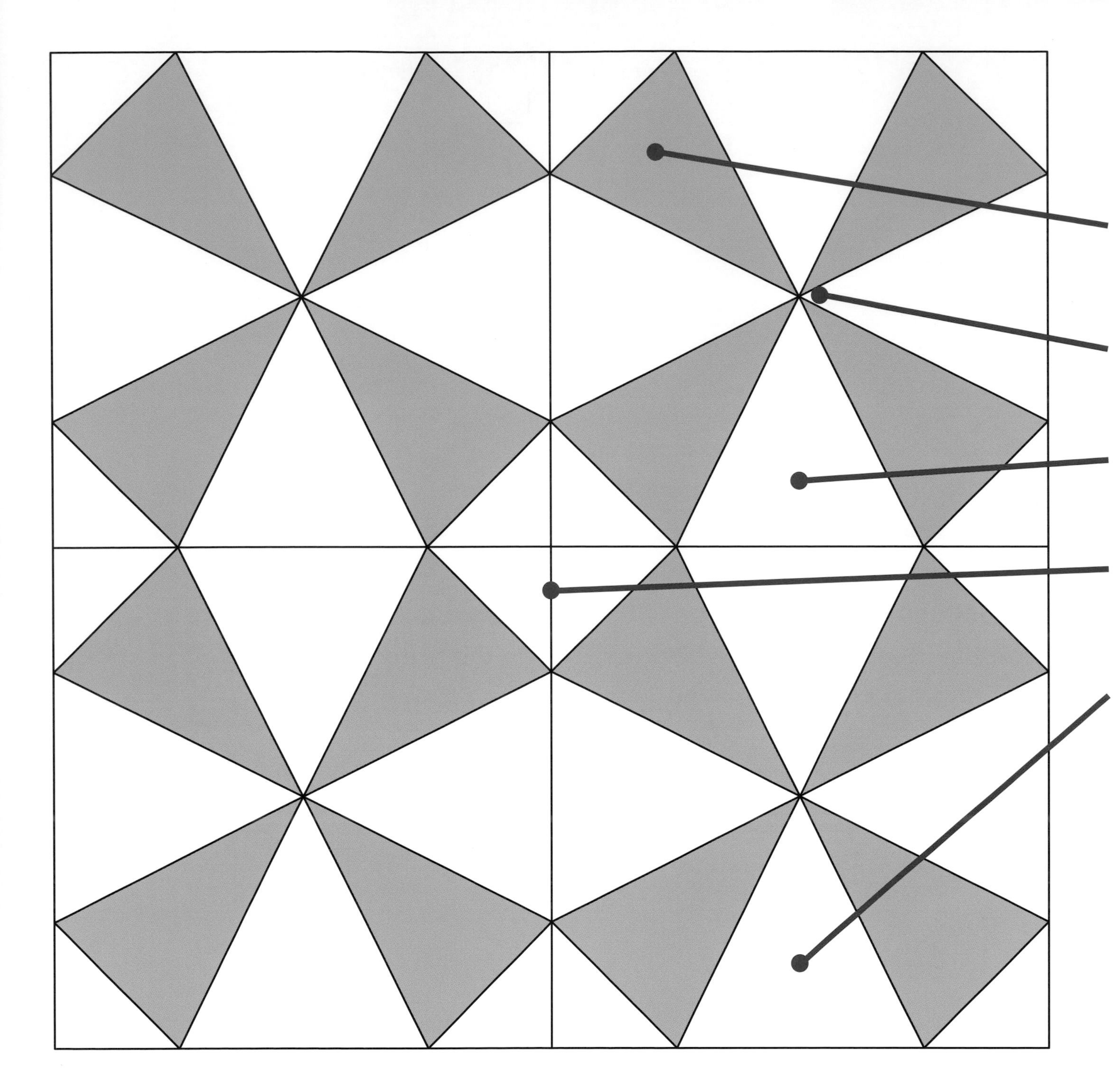

Kaleidoscope

The Kaleidoscope, and other star stackable patterns, are usually pieced with bold and colorful fabric, so treat them with simple orange peel, spiral, or circle designs.

The Kaleidoscope pieces can have a different number of points. Remember to look for quilting designs with the same number of points.

In the background areas around the Kaleidoscope stars, the negative space, stitching is especially visible on plain fabric.

It can be very effective when the quilting pattern extends into the Kaleidoscope block, ignoring the block seams.

Kaleidoscope quilting patterns usually are designed for the star itself, but consider placing the patterns in the background area that surrounds the design instead.

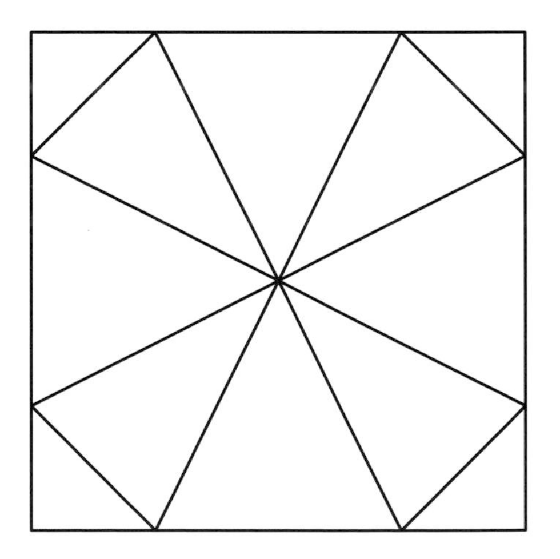

Log Cabin

The Log Cabin design is incredibly versatile with placements and colors. However, with such a large variety of block arrangements, it is not an easy pattern to quilt.

Stitching your way out from the center square with continuous-line motifs does not require precise perfection.

Look for quilting patterns that will enhance the zig-zag shape of the Log Cabin blocks.

Stitching-in-the-ditch with reflective decorative metallic threads or Mylar holographic ribbon looks great!

An undulating continuous-line vine of feathers, leaves, curls, plumes, and ribbons can gracefully wind its way through the lighter side of the Log Cabin setting.

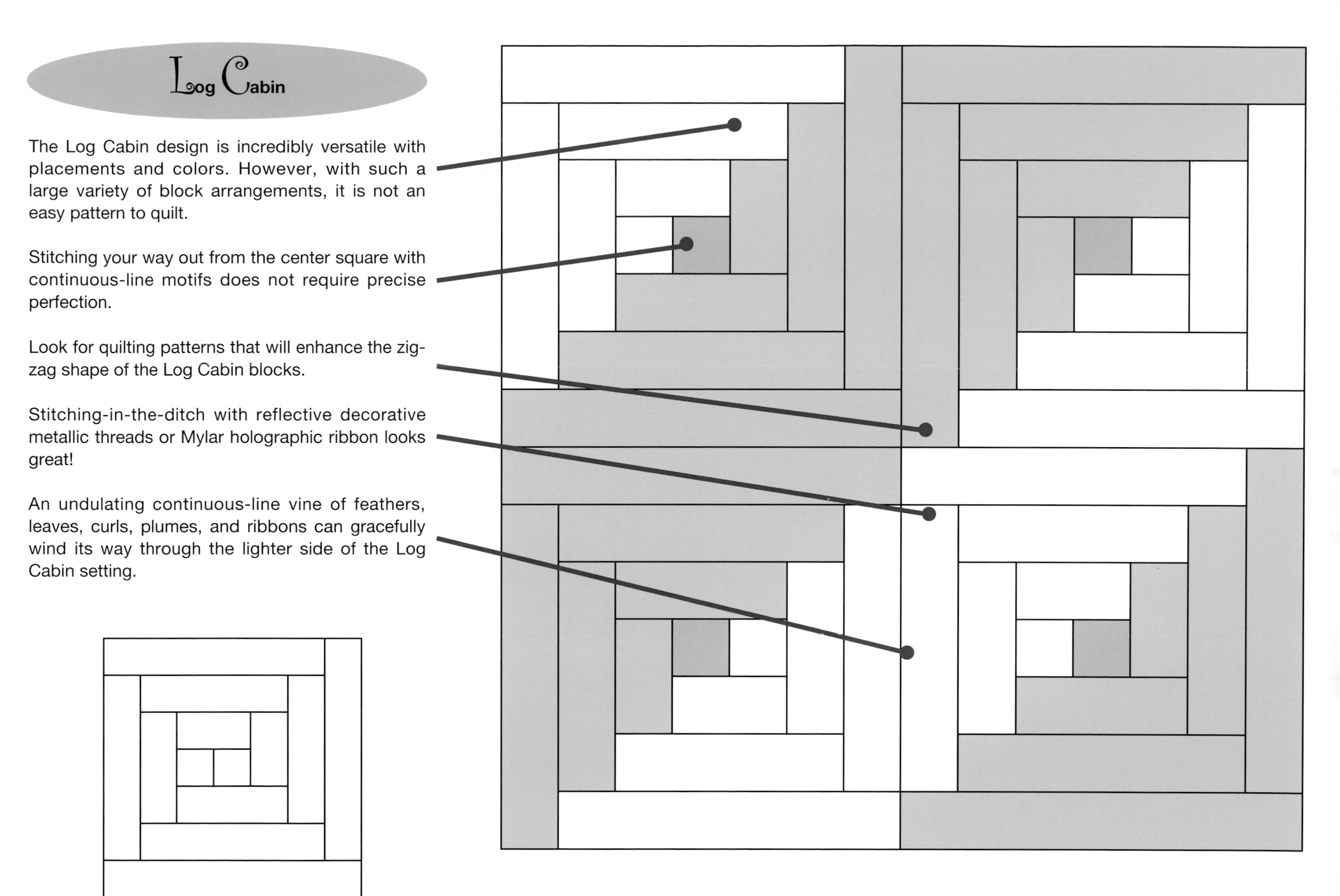

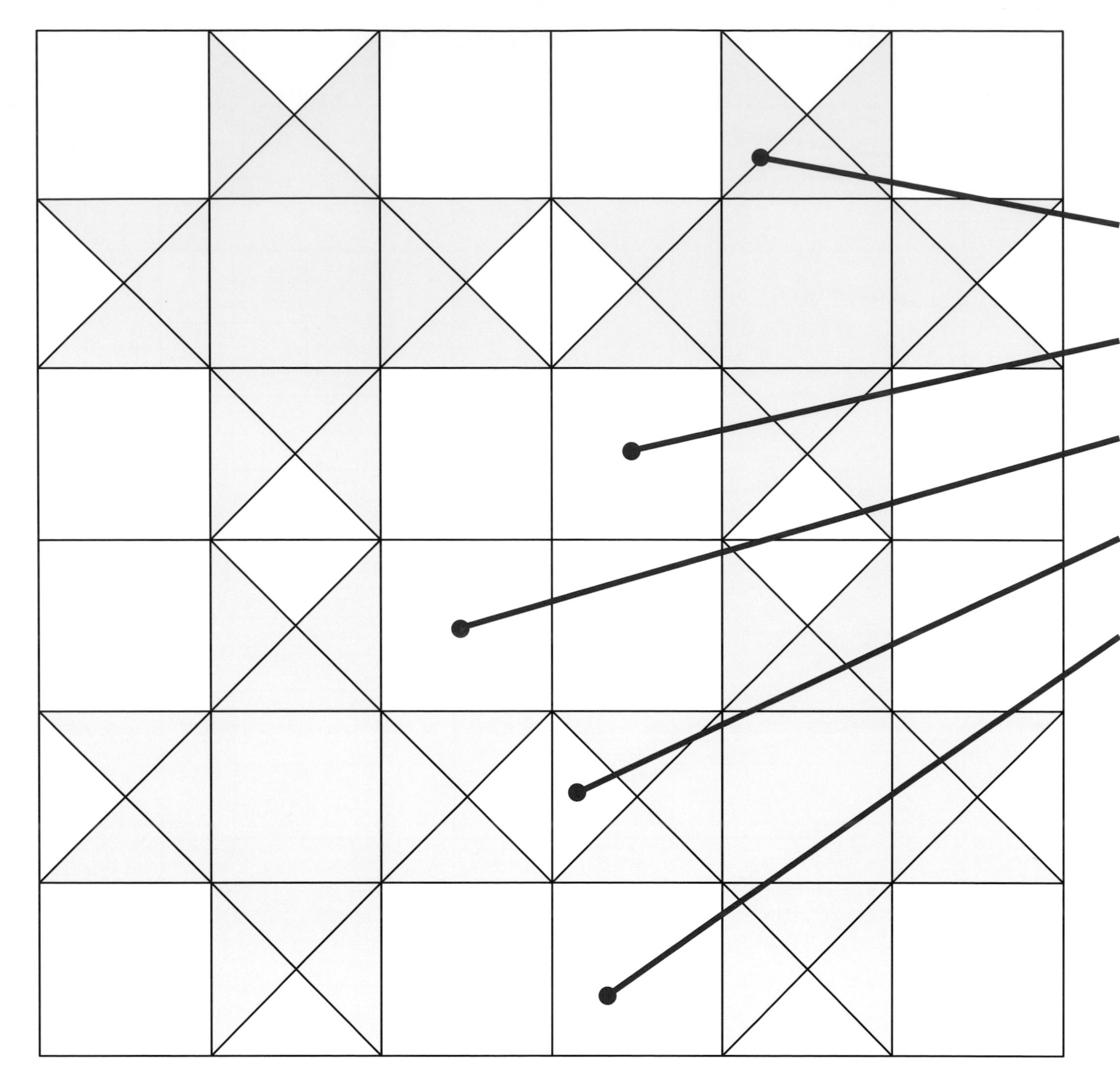

Star

Stitching-in-the-ditch along the main diagonal lines to form a larger "X." You could develop these lines even further for a more intricate secondary pattern.

The new area created can be quilted with a larger undulating, continuous-line pattern.

To give it some zip, consider placing a medallion or fancy quilting motif inside the area formed by the squares at the intersection.

Use a dense fill pattern, or meander, to minimize and flatten the background behind the stars.

To coordinate the pieces that appear next to the borders, repeat the main quilting motif, but use only half the design.

Choosing a decorative thread will add extra interest to any area.

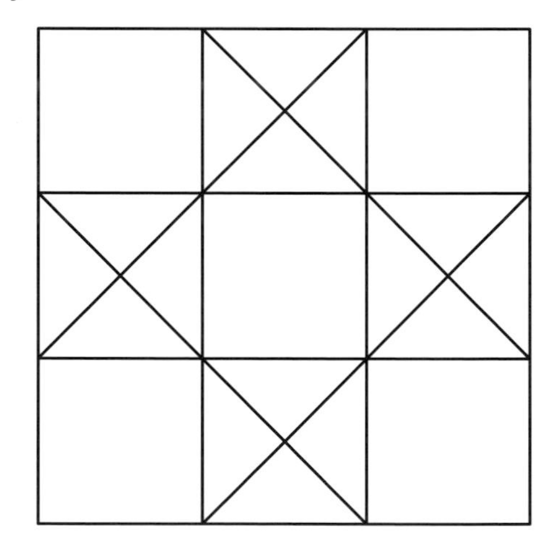

Bear Paw

Instead of quilting-in-the-ditch, use continuous S-curve quilting inside the small triangles.

A simple elementary quilting design of one flowing motif can be repeated in each paw.

For the sashing strips, choose a simple contrasing geometric line that will accent the curved-line quilting.

The wonderful Flying Geese pattern that is developing here can be quilted with a fill pattern in variegated thread.

To make paw pattern continuous through the center of the sashing use an interesting pattern that overlaps the center squares of the paw.

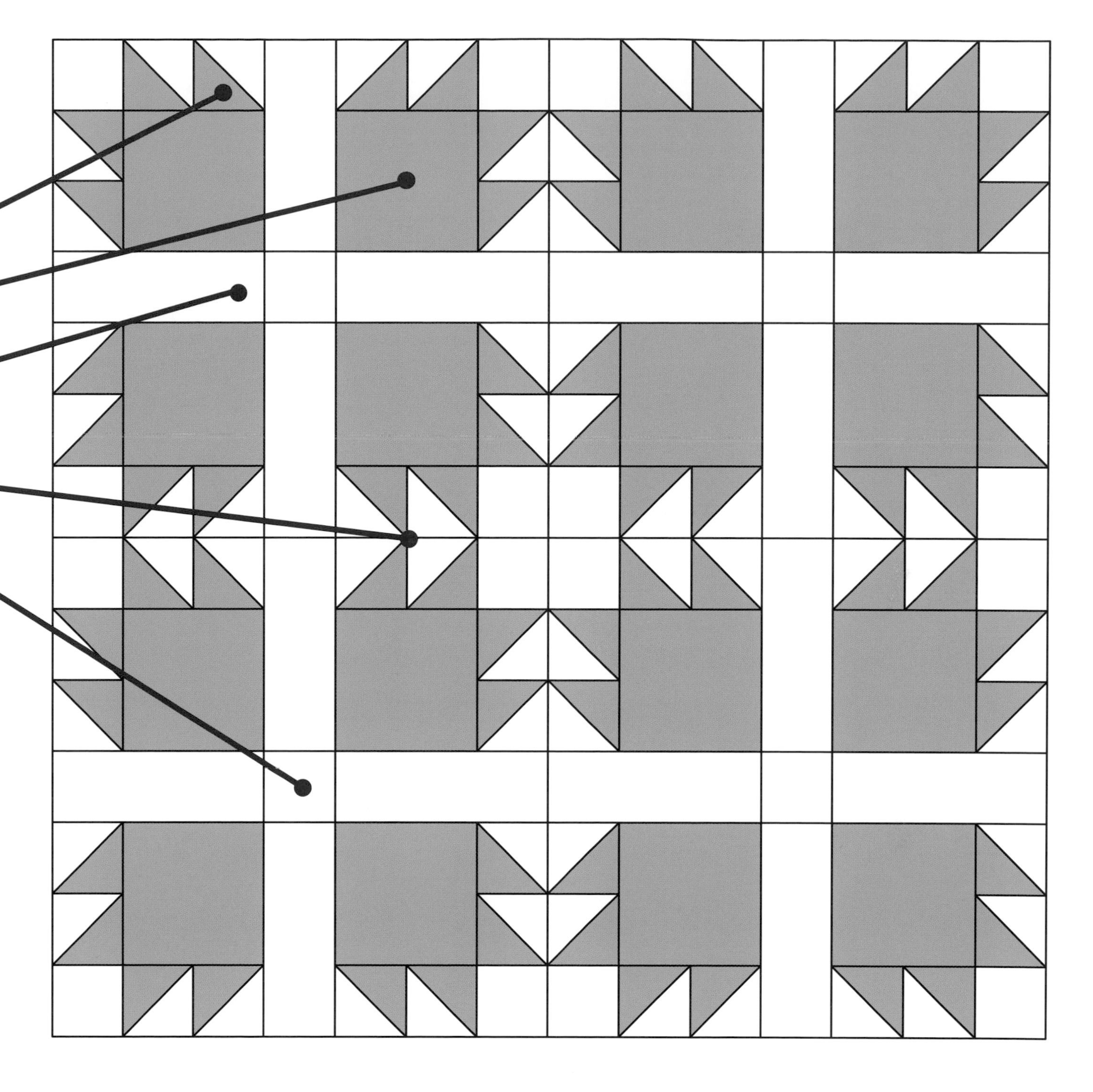

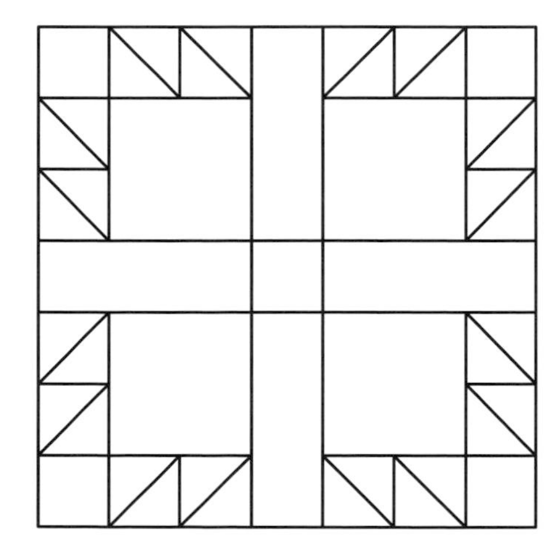

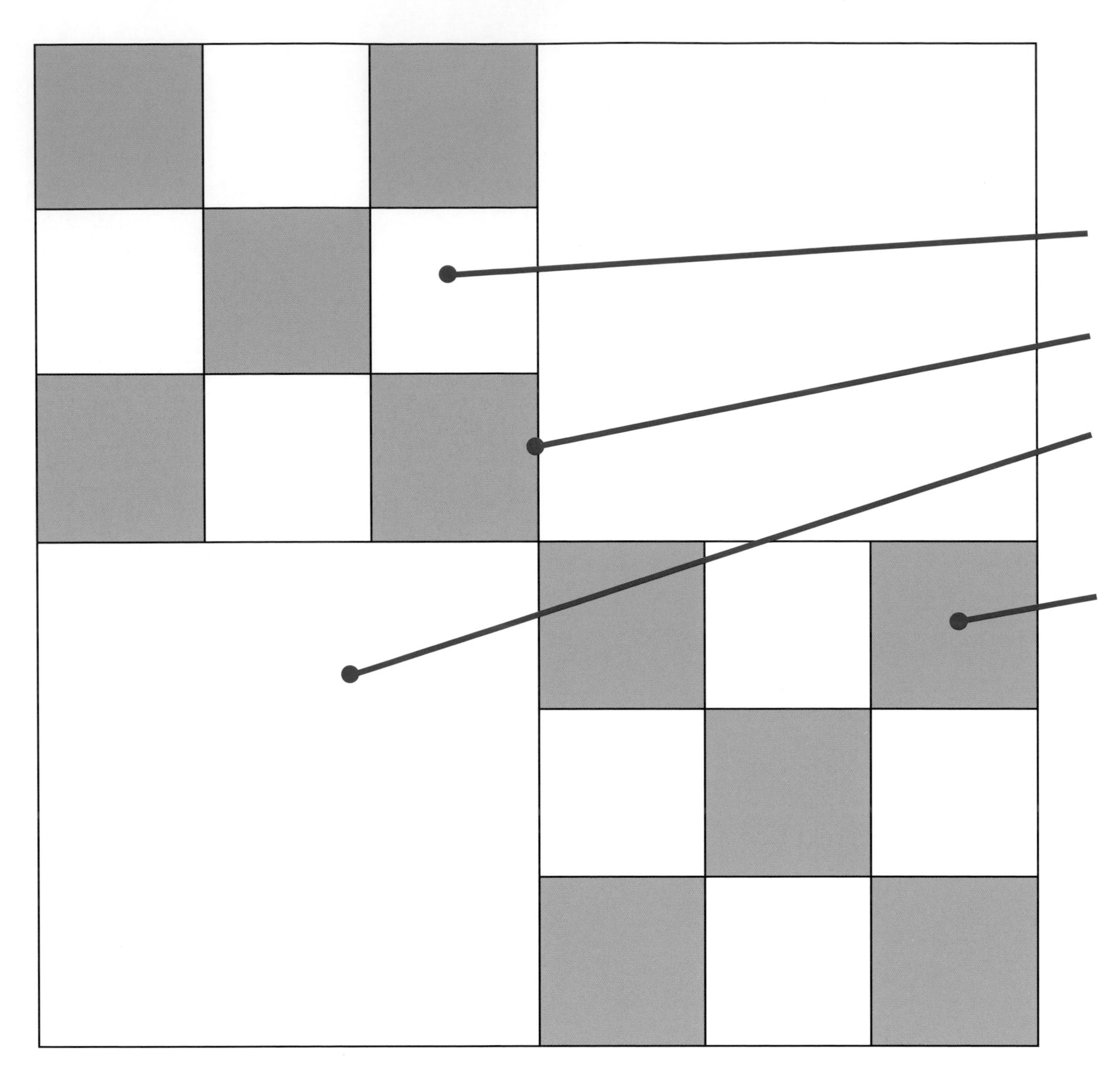

Nine-Patch

Most of the time, the Nine-Patch is used as an alternating square in a quilt. When the same shape is multiplied over and over in the blocks, the eye cannot focus on the overall design.

Quilting-in-the-ditch may not be the best choice for hard-edge block patterns.

A circular quilting pattern can be used in the larger plain block. This is the perfect place to showcase a fancy quilting design or secondary pattern.

A great way to quilt the Nine-Patch squares is to use what I call the "Terry Twist." This is a pattern of continuous line S-curves that outline the appropriate squares. It's easy to quilt and enhances the design. The undulating lines in Terry's Twist, shown below, provide movement and interest.

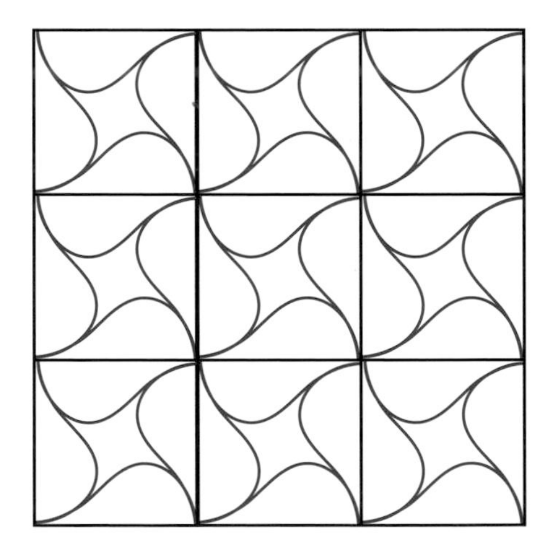

Sampler

As we discussed earlier, the sampler quilt needs to have the similar elements in each block treated alike. Some blocks in a sampler quilt may have a shape that is not contained in the other blocks. By quilting the common shape (i.e., triangle) into that block, you will be able to unite sampler blocks.

Treat the background around the various block patterns the same in every block.

Find the secondary design and treat it the same in every block.

The Bow Tie block, located in the lower right corner of the illustration, is a good example. You may wish to divide the center diamond through the middle and make two triangles. Imagine what you will come up with – there are so many possibilities that you will be amazed.

Find the common patch shapes in each sampler block, and design a uniform stitching pattern for each element. You may have to change thread color, or use a variegated thread to blend with all the fabric colors in the quilt top.

Pick out a fabric pattern or quilting motif and adapt it for the border design.

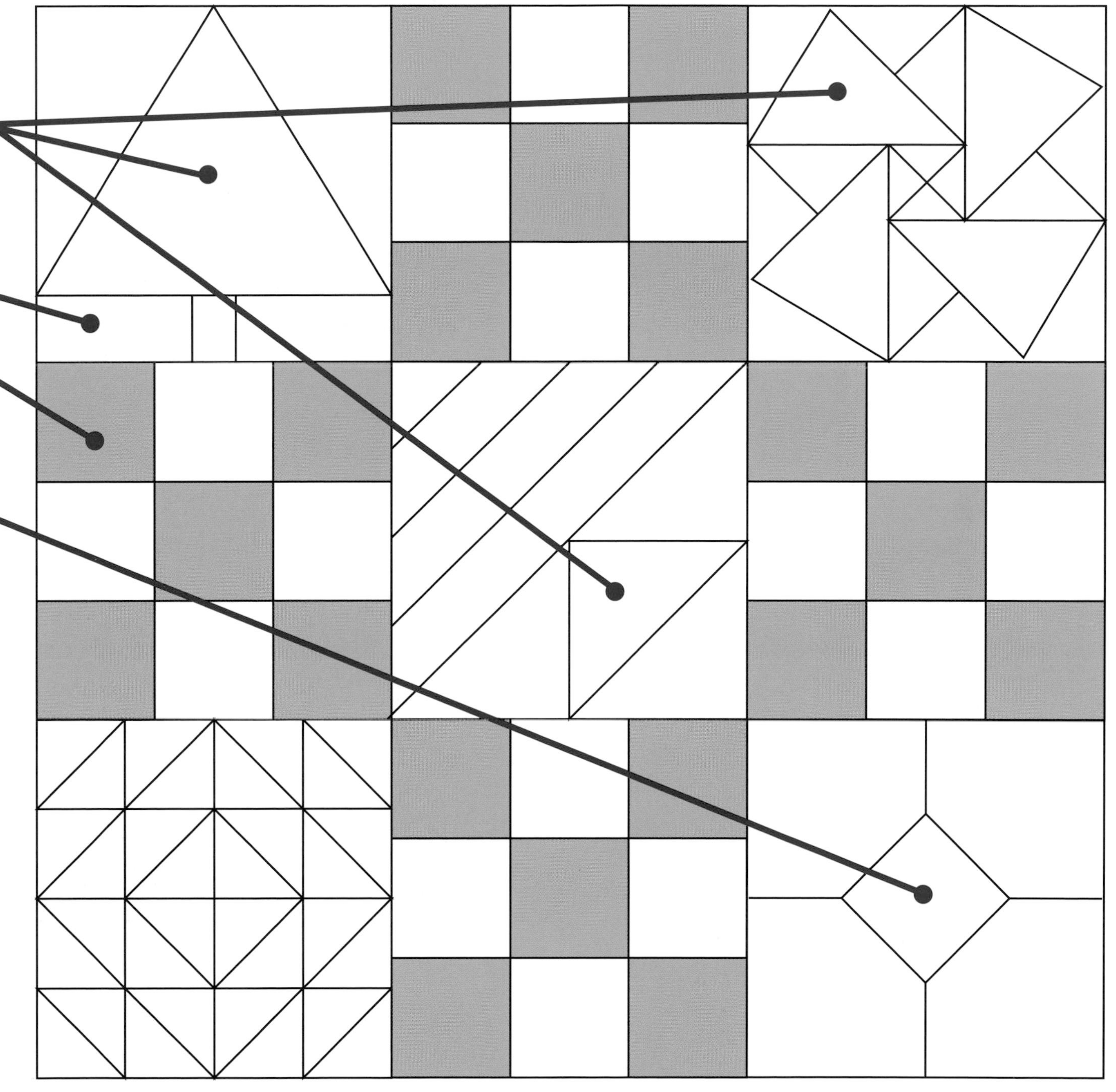

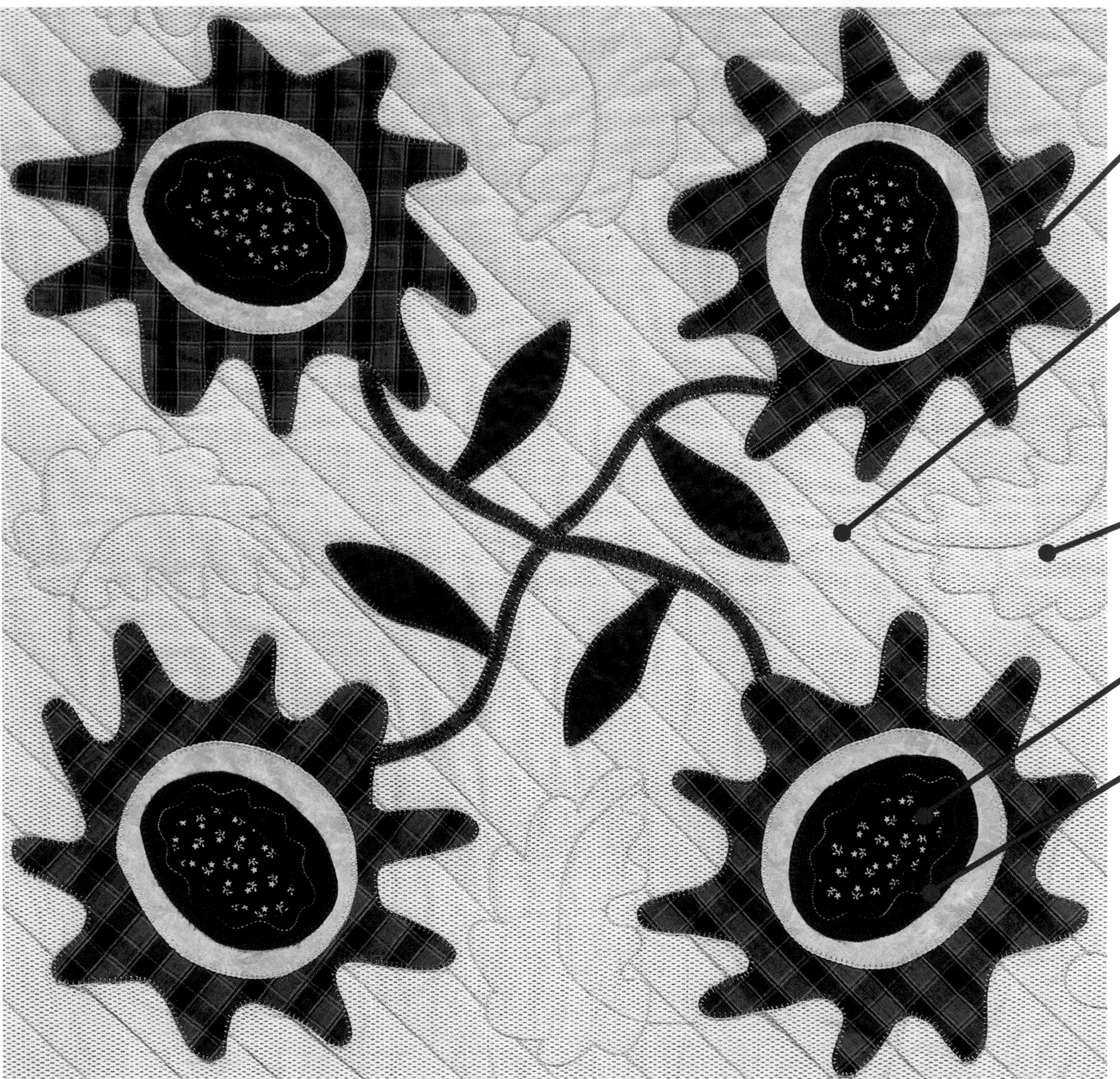

Appliqué

It is best to outline right next to the appliquéd shape.

Most appliqué is curved, so a good straight-line background filler is the railroad pattern. This is a pair of parallel lines ¼" apart, repeated every inch across the quilt. Railroad is easy to execute on any style of sewing machine and it is as distinctive as crosshatch, checkerboard or evenly spaced parallel lines.

To make your work easier, place a small motif to break up parallel lines where you would need to advance the quilt on a frame or to break long continuing straight lines when using a traditional machine.

Go back in with small motifs on the actual appliqué if the shape is too large to remain unquilted.

Choose variegated thread for the entire quilt instead of changing thread constantly.

Detail from quilt made by Desirée Clausen. Quilted by Sally Terry.

Embroidered

Quilt a continuous-line feather or motif fill within ¼" of embroidery.

Use large traditional patterns to anchor quilt sashings and in the borders to contrast with intricate embroidery.

Outline sashings and blocks or stitch-in-the-ditch to anchor squares. Use undulating lines instead of straight lines.

Traditional embroidered quilts usually have white or cream for stitching paths. Consider using a pastel variegated thread in the border that is in the same color family as the embroidery,

In small areas use crosshatching or curved web shapes.

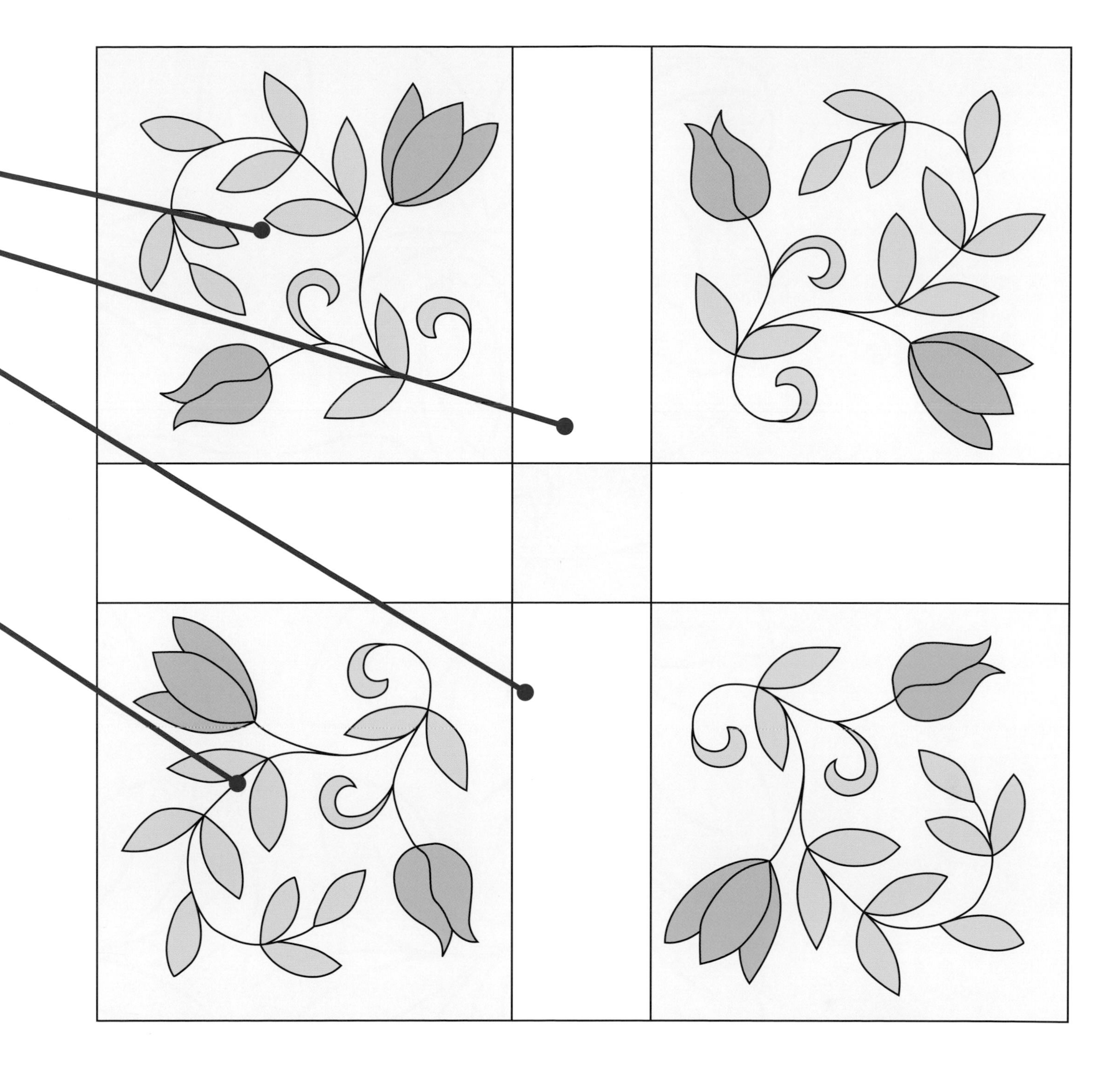

Appendix A

Dividing Spaces Equally. You can divide an area into any number of equal sections without using a calculator. All you need is a ruler – 18" long is ideal. It takes a little concentration the first time you use this method, but soon it will become second nature. Practice it several times and you will quickly become comfortable using this technique.

Find the two parallel lines that define the area you wish to divide. These are Line 1 and Line 2; they represent the inner and outer edges of a border.

Determine the number of equal spaces you need. In our example, we want to divide the area into four spaces.

Place the 0" mark of a ruler somewhere on Line 1.

Place a number that is divisible by the number of spaces desired on the opposite parallel line. In figure 1, the 4" mark is on Line 2.

Next, divide the last number on the ruler by the number of equal spaces you want. Four divided by 4 equals 1, so we marked every 1" along the ruler, placing marks at the 1", 2", and 3" markings.

Now draw lines through the markings that are parallel to the two sides (Line 1 and Line 2). You will have four equal spaces, as in figure 2.

If you want to divide a square, like the center square of a block, divide the square in one direction first, paying careful attention to which pair of parallel lines you

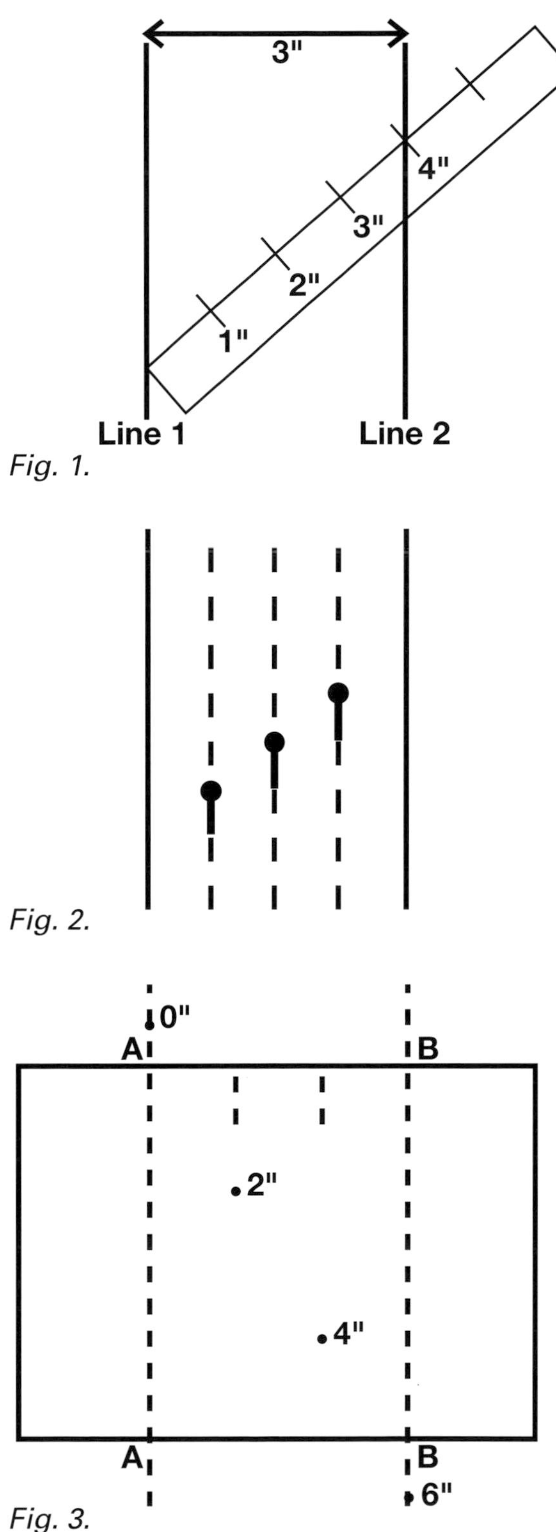

Fig. 1.

Fig. 2.

Fig. 3.

are working with; then divide the square in the other direction, using the parallel lines that go in the opposite direction.

If the space you are working with is too small for the required numbers on the ruler to fit within the unit, you can extend the parallel lines so that the ruler fits.

In figure 3, we needed three equal spaces between the parallel lines. By placing the 0" mark on Line A, and the 6" mark on Line B (3 spaces x 2" per space = 6"), the markings at 2" and 4" show where the equal divisions will be. Because the marks would not fit within the square, we extended boundary lines A and B beyond the original unit until the measurements on the ruler fit between the parallel lines.

Although the ruler is at an angle to the lines you are dividing, it still divides the space equally. This is a basic drafting technique for dividing a space, and you can use it for drafting blocks, as well as dividing spaces for quilting. Use it to mark the sides of corners and setting triangles to fan out lines evenly from a center point, as in figure 4.

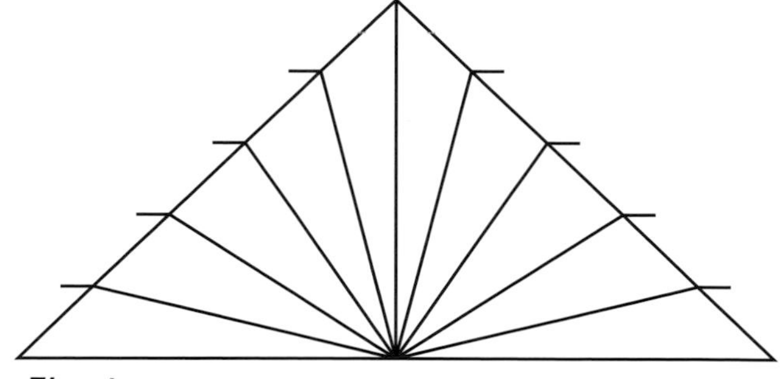
Fig. 4.

How To Set Up a Pantograph. I recommend two professional products: Quilts Complete sells a pantograph planner on their Web site at www.quiltscomplete.com. In addition, at the time of publication, Quilts Complete has a pantograph calculator on the Web site that is free to use, along with helpful information and instructions.

Spread the quilt out so you can easily mark the center each pantograph row on the quilt edge where the stitching will start. I usually use the back of the longarm table or the floor. I prefer to premark rather than mark as I go. I have not been accurate if I mark as I go.

16 Steps to Using a Pantograph. All measurements are from the center of the pantograph pattern.

1. Decide in which direction the pantograph is stitched to the quilt. There are new vertical pantographs available which give us even more of a choice and the quilt will be mounted side to side rather than top to bottom.

2. Measure the vertical distance between the highest and lowest point of a single row of the pantograph pattern. They will not usually be in the same area of the design.

3. Divide the measurement by two and mark the true horizontal center of your pantograph rows. If the rows interlock, mark their centers as well.

4. Remember the "rule of thumb" for the distance between the rows is your thumb. (Coined by Judy Allen.) Add half of the vertical measurement to a thumb's width (7/8"–1") for your first and last row center placement. Divide the distance between the pins by the vertical measurement that includes a thumb's width.

5. Use gold safety pins and pin every center mark for each row. If the measurement of the distance between the rows is more than 1" of the measurement of the pantograph including the 1" "rule of thumb," you may wish to consider using another size of pantograph pattern. Remember, the quilt will tell you where it needs quilting because it will be sloppy and puffy and not have the same overall texture as the rest of the quilt.

6. Mount the quilt and square up the top edge for quilting.

7. Walk the machine stylus or laser light from one edge of the quilt to the opposite edge and mark the two side edges on the panto with a non-permanent mark, with colorful cling tape, low-tack masking tape, or dry- or wet-erase marking pen. Usually the pantograph is beneath a plastic covering, so you will not be marking directly on the pantograph. Because the stylus or laser light arm extends out from the machine head, the start and stop boundaries are different on the back of the table and do not line up directly with the quilt. It is important to mark so you will know the proper relationship for starts and stops.

8. To find out where the pattern starts and stops on the quilt top I use calculator tape. Cut it to the correct length of the row and move it back and forth over the pattern until you are happy with the pattern as it relates to both outer edges of the quilt. If you are doing a border, make sure the quilt is straight or the stitching will drift up and down along its length. Measure the center of the border about every 10" and mark. Next, line the border center marks up with the center of the pantograph pattern. Tape the pantograph so the centers line up and it will not move, so the design stays consistently in the middle of the border area. Be sure to account for a ½" binding margin.

9. To turn a corner, locate and mark the natural 45-degree miter of the border corner. Keep in mind the ½" binding margin. Line up the top and bottom of the 45-degree corner of the pattern with the stylus or laser light. Tape down the pattern and stitch. It is best to start in an undetectable area such as an intersection or junction. Start stitching up through one pattern preceding the corner turn, continue through the corner, across the top and around the opposite corner, and down through one pattern stopping in an intersection or junction.

10. To fit the pattern or eliminate unnecessary lines, mark on the plastic cover with a non-permanent marker, or tape Golden Threads Quilting Paper over the pantograph and redraw.

11. Place the needle at the first pin and position the stylus or laser light on the center mark of the pantograph, where you marked the quilt edge on the pantograph plastic.

12. Move the needle to the quilt edge and begin stitching.

13. After stitching the row, position the needle back over the safety pin of the row you have just completed and advance the quilt so the next gold safety pin is directly under the needle. You will not need to reposition the stylus or laser light. Move the machine to the edge of the quilt and start stitching the design. For interlocking patterns, work off the center of the row as you did on a single row.

14. When you need to center a pantograph pattern on the quilt top, do the following: Move the machine head and line up the needle with the horizontal center of the quilt. Position the stylus or laser light on the horizontal and vertical center of pantograph design. Then move the machine to the edge and start quilting the first row from the gold safety pin.

15. Colorado Quilting Company makes The PatternGrid to make pantographs easier to use and placement more accurate. It is 12 feet long and fits on the table. Place the pattern under the grid. See Resources, page 93, for more information.

16. To elongate or shorten a pantograph to fit, find a point on the pantograph that will make the transition less noticeable. Measure the distance needed to shorten or elongate and divide it by the number of transition areas (typically they are between each repeat). Using that distance, move the laser, not the machine, to the right to elongate and to the left to shorten.

Resources

TEACHER, QUILTER, DESIGNER

Sally Terry
4300 Lovelaceville Road #178
Paducah, Kentucky 42001
e-mail: quiltershand@aol.com

Videos: *Creative Thread Guide*
Care and Adjustments: Longarm Quilting Machine
Getting Ready To Quilt

Pattern Packs: Fleur De Vine Pattern Pack
Graceful Victorian Designs

Pantographs: Fleur De Vine

FABRIC

Bruce Magidson
Firefly, LLC
719 Bennett St.
Portland, ND 58274
1-701-788-5556
www.sewbatik.com

Product: Batik Fabric 108" wide

GRIDS

Colorado Quilting Co, LLC
36159 Winchester Road
Elizabeth, CO 80107
1-303-646-9569

Products: The PatternGrid for Pantographs

PATTERNS

Jo Ann Belling
www.joannbelling.com
WHIMSICAL TRIANGLES, page 61

Maple Island Quilts
Debbie Bowles
www.mapleislandquilts.com
EUREKA, page 47

PUBLISHERS, SUPPLIES

Golden Threads
2 S 373 Seneca Drive
Wheaton, Illinois 60187
www.goldenthreads.com
1-888-477-7718

THREAD

Robison-Anton Textile Co.
175 Bergen Blvd.
Fairview, NJ 07022
1-201-941-0500
e-mail: chorvath@ robison-anton.com

Products: Rayon and polyester embroidery threads; metallic, cotton, and polyester

THREAD

Superior Threads
PO Box 1672
St. George, UT 84771
1-435-652-1867
e-mail: info@superiorthreads.com

Products: Superior Metallic™ threads, Glitter™ hologram

Bibliography

Benvin, Roberta. *Antique Quilting Designs*. Kentucky: American Quilter's Society, 2001.

Chainey, Barbara. *Quilt It*. Washington: Martingale & Co., 1999.

Cory, Pepper. *Mastering Quilt Marking*. California: C&T Publishing, Inc., 1996.

Terry, Sally. *Fleur De Vine Pattern Pack*. Illinois: Golden Threads, 2002.

Terry, Sally. *Heart of Creative Quilting*. Illinois: Powell Publishing, 2003.

Terry, Sally. *Language of Quilting*. Illinois: Golden Threads, 2003.

Thompson, Shauna. *Distinctive Designs in Continuous Line*. Illinois: Powell Publications, 2000.

Thompson, Shirley. *Think Small*. Illinois: Powell Publications, 1990.

Thompson, Shirley. *Designs for Continuous Line Quilting.* Illinois: Powell Publications, 1993.

The *Language of Quilting* and my techniques will enable you to develop your own style. You do not have to copy me! In addition, you will have the tools you need to take any class, basic to advanced, and feel confident about the outcome. Furthermore, you will be able use the most complex of patterns with ease. This is not a book about making something just as I did to make it look good. It is all about taking your own style and making it look so good that all your shapes will be beautiful.

You have finished the *Pathways to Better Quilting*. Please raise your right hand and take the machine quilter's oath. It is my wish that there is another quilter somewhere taking the oath with you at the same time. Imagine that!

The Machine Quilters' Oath

Raise your right hand.

"I ______________________________, can machine quilt.

I will approach my machine with confidence and dignity.

I will give my machine a loving name and all the oil it wants.

I will not be afraid to try.

I will enjoy the process.

I will become the Quilter I want to be."

About The Author

Sally Terry's quiltmaking path began at the age of three. Throughout her childhood, she made all her own clothing and even tailored her own suits. At high school graduation, the only clothes in her closet that she had not made were a jacket, a pair of denims, and a bathing suit. Her only lament is that she never got to shop for clothes.

After graduating from Drake University, Sally attended graduate school in multimedia at the University of Grenoble in France. Her interest in making batiks developed at this time and she recalls her house reeking from melted crayons. Sally also developed a passion for intense, light-up-your-life color.

Her interest and background in marketing made it easy for Sally to start a home-based quilting business in Iowa called The Quilter's Hand. There, she found her niché through the challenge of developing quilting designs for creative quilts. Her enthusiasm for quilting has resulted in a professional design and teaching career, allowing her to enthusiastically share her vast knowledge.

Sally's ideas have been published in quilting magazines and books and taught throughout the United States and Canada at quilt shows, workshops, and guilds. She is enrolled in the Janome Instructor Program and teaches for the Janome Institute. Her lectures are based on why particular designs and techniques work. She teaches concepts that are easily understood and mastered.

Since 2000, Sally has demonstrated and sold longarm machines. She is a quilting designer with Golden Threads, has three videos on longarm quilting, and has made numerous guest appearances on television quilting shows. A new resident of Paducah, Kentucky, Sally lived in Des Moines, Iowa, for over 20 years.

Yours in the love of quilting

This is only a small selection of the books and CDs available from the American Quilter's Society.
AQS books are known worldwide for timely topics,
clear writing, beautiful color photos, and for accurate illustrations and patterns.
The following books are available from your local bookseller or quilt shop.

LOOK for these books nationally. CALL 1-800-626-5420
or VISIT our Website at www.AmericanQuilter.com